Asian Genders in Tourism

ASPECTS OF TOURISM

***Series Editors*: Chris Cooper** *(Oxford Brookes University, UK)*, **C. Michael Hall** *(University of Canterbury, New Zealand)* and **Dallen J. Timothy** *(Arizona State University, USA)*

Aspects of Tourism is an innovative, multifaceted series, which comprises authoritative reference handbooks on global tourism regions, research volumes, texts and monographs. It is designed to provide readers with the latest thinking on tourism worldwide and push back the frontiers of tourism knowledge. The volumes are authoritative, readable and user-friendly, providing accessible sources for further research. Books in the series are commissioned to probe the relationship between tourism and cognate subject areas such as strategy, development, retailing, sport and environmental studies.

Full details of all the books in this series and of all our other publications can be found on http://www.channelviewpublications.com, or by writing to Channel View Publications, St Nicholas House, 31-34 High Street, Bristol BS1 2AW, UK.

ASPECTS OF TOURISM: 75

Asian Genders in Tourism

Edited by
Catheryn Khoo-Lattimore and Paolo Mura

CHANNEL VIEW PUBLICATIONS
Bristol • Buffalo • Toronto

Library of Congress Cataloging in Publication Data
A catalog record for this book is available from the Library of Congress.
Names: Khoo-Lattimore, Catheryn, – editor. | Mura, Paolo Biagio, editor.
Title: Asian Genders in Tourism/Edited by Catheryn Khoo-Lattimore and Paolo Mura.
Description: Bristol, UK; Tonawanda, NY: Channel View Publications, [2016]
 | Series: Aspects of Tourism: 75 |
Includes bibliographical references and index.
Identifiers: LCCN 2016022062| ISBN 9781845415792 (hbk : alk. paper) |
 ISBN 9781845415785 (pbk : alk. paper) | ISBN 9781845415822 (Kindle) | ISBN 9781845415808 (Pdf) | ISBN 9781845415815 (Epub)
Subjects: LCSH: Tourism--Social aspects--Asia. | Sex role--Asia. | Asians--Ethnic identity.
Classification: LCC G155.A74 A86 2016 | DDC 306.4/819081095--dc23 LC record available at https://lccn.loc.gov/2016022062

British Library Cataloguing in Publication Data
A catalogue entry for this book is available from the British Library.

ISBN-13: 978-1-84541-579-2 (hbk)
ISBN-13: 978-1-84541-578-5 (pbk)

Channel View Publications
UK: St Nicholas House, 31-34 High Street, Bristol BS1 2AW, UK.
USA: UTP, 2250 Military Road, Tonawanda, NY 14150, USA.
Canada: UTP, 5201 Dufferin Street, North York, Ontario M3H 5T8, Canada.

Website: www.channelviewpublications.com
Twitter: Channel_View
Facebook: https://www.facebook.com/channelviewpublications
Blog: www.channelviewpublications.wordpress.com

Copyright © 2016 Catheryn Khoo-Lattimore, Paolo Mura and the authors of individual chapters.

All rights reserved. No part of this work may be reproduced in any form or by any means without permission in writing from the publisher.

The policy of Multilingual Matters/Channel View Publications is to use papers that are natural, renewable and recyclable products, made from wood grown in sustainable forests. In the manufacturing process of our books, and to further support our policy, preference is given to printers that have FSC and PEFC Chain of Custody certification. The FSC and/or PEFC logos will appear on those books where full certification has been granted to the printer concerned.

Typeset by R. J. Footring Ltd, Derby

Contents

Acknowledgements		vii
Contributors		ix
1	The Embodiment of Gender and 'Asianness' in Tourism *Catheryn Khoo-Lattimore and Paolo Mura*	1
2	Asian Gendered Identities in Tourism *Elaine Chiao Ling Yang and Paolo Mura*	6
3	'Doing' Tourism Gender Research in Asia: An Analysis of Authorship, Research Topic and Methodology *Elaine Chiao Ling Yang and Rokhshad Tavakoli*	23
4	Asian Gendered Performance in Tourism *Tau Sian Lim and Paolo Mura*	40
5	The Impact of Masculinities in the Researcher–Respondent Relationship: A Socio-Historical Perspective *Karun Rawat and Catheryn Khoo-Lattimore*	53
6	The Asian Female Tourist Gaze: A Conceptual Framework *Eunice Tan and Barkathunnisha Abu Bakar*	65
7	'Home' as a Mobile Cultural Diaspora: South Asian American Women and the Conceptualisation of Holidays in America *Roksana Badruddoja*	88
8	My Journeys in Second Life: An Autonetnography *Rokhshad Tavakoli*	104

9 Conclusion 121
   Paolo Mura and Catheryn Khoo-Lattimore

Index 126

Acknowledgements

The production of this book was made possible by a much appreciated grant from the Griffith Institute for Tourism (GIFT). We are also grateful to Mun Yee Lai and Mona Jihyun Yang, both from Griffith University, for their administrative assistance during the final stages of this book. We thank the chapter contributors for their optimism, hard work and perseverance to work through multiple drafts of their manuscripts. We would also like to express gratitude for the collegiality of the reviewers, who offered constructive comments on the content and provided support for the book.

This book is the result of countless hours in isolation, away from our loved ones. We are thankful to our partners and immediate family members, whose understanding and selflessness were critical to the completion of this book.

Catheryn Khoo-Lattimore
Griffith University, Australia

Paolo Mura
Taylor's University, Malaysia

Contributors

Editors

Catheryn Khoo-Lattimore holds a PhD in Consumer Behaviour from the University of Otago, New Zealand, and has worked in Malaysia, the United States and now Australia. She was a 2013/14 Fulbright Scholar with residency at the University of Florida, and is now a senior lecturer in the Department of Tourism, Sport and Hotel Management at Griffith University. Catheryn's current research interest is on tourist and guest behaviour, with a passionate focus on women, families and young children. She is also particularly interested in understanding these segments from an Asian perspective, and how their travel experience and behaviours differ cross-culturally. Catheryn serves on the editorial boards of the *Journal of Hospitality and Tourism Education*, the *Journal of Hospitality and Tourism Management*, *Tourism Review* and *Anatolia*. She is an executive committee member of the Council for Australasian Tourism and Hospitality Education (CAUTHE) and board member of the Asia Pacific Council on Hotel, Restaurant, and Institutional Education (APacCHRIE). She is also the founder and chair of Women Academics in Tourism (WAiT). Catheryn lives in a bayside suburb with her husband and their three young children, and attempts furniture upcycling in her spare time, when she can find any.

Paolo Mura holds a PhD in Tourism from the University of Otago, New Zealand. An Italian by passport, he has lived in Germany, the United States, New Zealand and Malaysia. He is currently a Senior Lecturer and Programme Director of the Postgraduate Programmes in the School of Hospitality, Tourism and Culinary Arts at Taylor's University, Malaysia. Overall, his research interests are on tourist behaviour, with a focus on young tourists' experiences, gender, qualitative methodologies, and Asia. Paolo serves on the editorial board of *Current Issues in Tourism*, *Journal of Vacation Marketing*, the

Annals of Leisure Research and *Asia Pacific Journal of Innovation in Hospitality and Tourism*.

Authors

Roksana is a feminine and masculine woman, a Bangladeshi-American, a queer, a Muslim, a mother to a fierce 12-year-old girl who is negotiating her 'brownness' at school, and an Advanced Assistant Professor and Coordinator for Women's and Gender Studies (WAGS) at Manhattan College. She teaches courses on feminist research methods, women of colour in the United States, feminist activism, race and ethnicity, sociology of gender and representations of women. Her research in the areas of race and ethnicity, sexuality, gender, religion and culture, and how these impact South Asian American women, has been published in numerous peer-reviewed journals. She is the author of *Eyes of the Storms: The Voices of South Asian-American Women* and the editor of *'New Maternalisms': Tales of Mother (Dislodging the Unthinkable)*. She is also board member for the *Journal of the Motherhood Initiative (JMI)* and Council on Contemporary Families (CCF), as well as an Advisory Board Member for the Museum of Motherhood (MOM).

Karun has recently graduated with a Master of Science in Tourism from Taylor's University, Malaysia. His master's thesis focused on the integration of innovative approaches into community-based tourism. He has developed research interests that include qualitative research methodologies, community-based tourism, adventure tourism, innovation and rural tourism. He is currently involved in an UNWTO research report on the influence of destination marketing on small and medium enterprises in Yuntaishan, Henan Province, China.

Rokhshad has recently completed her doctoral studies in tourism at Taylor's University, Malaysia, and taken up a faculty position at Sunway University. Her PhD explored social capital within the context of Malaysian home-stays. Her research interests include tourist behaviour, gender, 2D and 3D social networks, virtual tourism, contemporary issues in tourism and ethnographic approaches to research.

Elaine's main area of interest is gender studies in tourism. Her doctoral research focuses on Asian solo female travellers and their perception of risk in the gendered and ethnicised tourism space. She is also currently involved in research on girlfriend get-away holidays. Her other research interests include qualitative research methodologies, postcolonial feminist research, Asian tourist behaviour, tourist risk perception and food studies.

Eunice Tan, DHTM, is the Managing Partner and Principal Consultant of Enseigner Consulting Asia LLP, and Associate Lecture at Murdoch University, Singapore. Her research interests are in sustainable tourism, tourism education and interpretation, volunteer tourism, cultural and culinary tourism.

Barkathunnisha is a Doctor of Philosophy (PhD) candidate at the School of Arts at Murdoch University (Western Australia), and Associate Lecturer at Murdoch University, Singapore. Her research interests are in tourism education, sustainable tourism, tourism marketing and cultural tourism.

Tau Sian is a PhD candidate in tourism and hospitality at Taylor's University, Malaysia. Tau Sian's PhD focuses on tourism and gender in Southeast Asia, using the covers of travel magazines as the focal point in understanding the postmodern Southeast Asian society. His research interests include gender, postmodernism and qualitative research methodologies, especially critical approaches to tourism and hospitality.

1 The Embodiment of Gender and 'Asianness' in Tourism

Catheryn Khoo-Lattimore and Paolo Mura

> *For some contemporary commentators, academic and activist discussions about 'gender' are 'so last century', a debate out of place in today's postmodern world....*
> (Pritchard *et al.*, 2007: 1)

> *... structural inequalities carry little weight, and concerns about the existence and consequences of social differences based on genders are seen to be 'politically old fashioned'.*
> (Oakley, 2006: 19)

Introduction

Despite the above sentiments, Pritchard *et al.* (2007) have emphasised the crucial need to continue gender-focused work in tourism. This work is even more pressing in Asia, and from an Asian perspective. As one of the largest tourist-receiving regions, with many emerging markets such as India and Southeast Asia (World Tourism Organization, 2015), Asia is increasingly become a promising market for tourism (Winter *et al.*, 2008). Considering the massive economic potential of tourism in the region, it is not surprising that tourism research in Asia has gained increasing scholarly attention. This new interest in tourism in Asia, however, is predominantly focused on business and marketing, and gender research on Asians as travellers and providers of tourism experiences has not caught up. Moreover, the landscape of the tourism academy is changing, as is the number of Asian researchers (Henderson & Gibson, 2013). A book addressing Asian gendered identities and tourism from a reflexive Asian-centric approach is very therefore timely, especially one with contributors with diverse Asian academic profiles (Mura & Pahlevan Sharif, 2015).

In this regard, we believe that the composition of the team of researchers who produced this book represents the uniqueness of this book, as the authors' work and leisure routines over time have been unconsciously (and maybe more consciously for some) based on understanding and negotiating both Western and Asian identities and practices. More specifically, the authors' academic and their equally important non-academic backgrounds and experiences will provide a balanced array of emic and etic perspectives necessary to understand in detail the complexities of gender in Asia. As the reflexivity of researchers as participants is increasingly encouraged, we feel that each author's 'situation' within their own chapters and topics discussed in the book adds a methodological dimension not discussed in any other books on gender. Given that this is the introductory chapter, we also introduce ourselves and the chapter authors to the reader as both researchers and 'bodies' located within the tourism topics discussed in this book. To this effect, we first introduce ourselves as editors of the book, and then the authors in the subsequent paragraphs.

Catheryn Khoo-Lattimore is a Malaysian female who has lived in Malaysia for most of her adult life and then pursued an academic career in New Zealand, Malaysia, the USA and Australia. Being married to a white New Zealander, her research often takes a cultural and gendered approach, comparing similarities and differences between Asians and their Western counterparts. Paolo Mura is an Italian male who has studied in Western countries (Italy, Germany, the USA and New Zealand) and has been working as a lecturer and researcher in Malaysia since 2010. In the last 10 years, Paolo's work has focused on gendered identities on holiday. His PhD studies explored young tourists' perceptions of fear from a gender perspective. At the moment, his research interests are centred on Asian gendered identities.

Asian Identities in Tourism

While it is easy to define Asia in terms of its geographical boundaries, characterising the diverse Asian identities and their cultural values is a much more difficult task. In Chapter 2, Elaine Chiao Ling Yang and Paolo Mura take on this task and discuss the socio-cultural construction of genders in Asia and what it is to be an Asian woman, man or 'other'. They examine Asian identities with reference to the dominant cultural ideologies practised in the region – Confucianism, Islam and Hinduism – and how these ideologies have affected the construction of not only gender norms but also socially accepted travel behaviour for contemporary Asian male and female travellers. These ideologies also form the three major religions embraced by Malaysians (Butler *et al.*, 2014), and Elaine, as a Malaysian Chinese, is well placed to provide an emic perspective on the topic in this chapter. As an avid female traveller, Elaine has first-hand experience of linking her doctoral work on Asian female solo travellers to her own experience as an objectified body in tourism. Paolo, an Italian living in Malaysia, contributes a somewhat etic view to this chapter.

Eight out of the 19 books we found in our initial research for competing titles (see below) take a more encompassing male–female approach in the discussion of gender in Asia. However, these books also adopt a very minimalist approach to gender, as they refer to gender using monolithic categories such as 'men' and 'women'. In doing so, existing work on gender in Asia reduces the complexity of gendered relationships to minimalist studies on women's experiences. In contrast, our book provides a different and complex analysis of gender-based relations in Asia. 'Gender', as it is used throughout this book, is not intended to refer only to one's biological sex (e.g. man or woman). Our aim from the beginnings of this book was to treat the term 'gender' as encompassing a more complex meaning, and as a sociocultural construct which regulates how men and women interact with each other in a wider social and tourism setting. We therefore introduce these Asian male–female interactions in a tourism setting in Chapter 4, where Tau Sian Lim and Paolo Mura discuss the concepts of 'performance' and 'performativity' from theatrical studies, cultural studies and anthropology. In doing so, Tau Sian reflects on his researcher identity as an Asian male exploring the embodiment and enactment of Asian femininity, through the performance of Asian women as tourists on a beach holiday. His reflexivity allows for an understanding of how different masculinities and femininities are performed in different contexts and how they interact to shape gender-based political and socio-cultural structures of power in Asia.

Who's Who in Asian Genders and Tourism Research?

When researching competing titles for this book, we entered keywords such as 'Asian + gender', 'Asia + gender' into major publishers' websites, Google Scholar and Google Books. Although not tourism focused, we did find 19 books on Asian gender and identities, but 11 of these focused on women. Cursory explorations into books that relate gender to tourism revealed interesting work by Kinnaird and Hall in 1994, Sinclair in 1997, Swain and Momsen in 2002, and Pritchard, Morgan, Ateljevic and Harris in 2007, but very few chapters in these books focus on Asian gendered identities in tourism, partly because many of the books' contributors are Western academics. In Chapter 3, Elaine Chiao Ling Yang and Rokhshad Tavakoli provide an analysis of how past studies have approached Asian genders and tourism. The chapter introduces the reader to the paradigms and methods used by past scholars in their work on tourism research in Asia. It presents both quantitative and qualitative methodologies before revealing the dearth of research on Asia, Asians and Asianness that embraces the crisis of representation. Both Elaine and Rokhshad are young Asian scholars, so their reflections on the issues of power relations in knowledge creation challenge us as a tourism academy to be more accessible to scholars who may not be proficient in the universal language of publications – that is, English – and to consider how the freedom of research is limited in some Asian countries. Their voices echo that of Khoo-Lattimore (2017), who laments the barriers placed in the way of Asian academics in their quest for academic excellence. As a result of their analysis, the authors of Chapter 3 recommend that tourism researchers adopt more critical and reflexive approaches, and find alternative, localised methods for producing knowledge.

As a response to Elaine and Rokhshad's chapter, Karun Rawat and Catheryn Khoo-Lattimore in Chapter 5 reflect on the dynamics of the Asian researcher–Asian respondent relationship, and in particular how the performance of masculinities among indigenous people in Asia might affect the quality of in-depth data collection. As Karun Rawat is a young Nepali male who has spent most of his life immersed in patriarchal societies with traditional stereotyped definitions of the roles of men and women, it is interesting to see the notion of masculinity in this chapter not only conceptualised within the male researcher's identity but also emerging among the female indigenous participants in the study presented in the chapter. This emergence, and the acknowledgement of it, reiterate the intersectionality of femininity and masculinity within genders, and in gender studies. At the end of the chapter, the authors come to the realisation that when analysed from a socio-historical point of view, the acquired researcher identity is closer to the socio-cultural identity of his participants than was originally assumed, and that this relationship plays a role in the data collection and analysis stages of any research.

In Chapter 6, Eunice Tan and Barkathunnisha Abu Bakar provide an insight into the Asian female tourist gaze. As Singaporean female tourism scholars, Eunice and Nisha challenge the universalism of the tourism gaze and highlight the cultural and gendered nature of the Asian female gaze. Importantly, by reiterating the idea that the tourist gaze has tended to privilege white males and ignore Asian tourists, their work reminds us of the academic structures of power underpinning tourism scholarly production.

In Chapter 7, Roksana Badruddoja explores the gendered identities of South Asian American women in negotiating their consumption and experiences of Western holidays in America. As a second-generation South Asian American herself, Roksana has had to battle her own different identities, so her own experiences were instrumental in writing this chapter. Likewise, in identifying herself with the 25 female participants of her year-long ethnographic study, she benefited from the acquisition of a calm confidence, understanding and acceptance that it is not possible for an immigrant to choose 'an' identity, because identities are fluid and need to be negotiated at all times. Roksana emphasises this point through Western holiday celebrations such as Christmas, which do not immediately and naturally align with the women's identity as South Asians, even when they do feel connected to such holidays as second-generation Americans. In her analysis, she discusses the intersections among women and their gendered identity, taking into account their skin colour, immigration status and diasporic movement, as well as national belonging and the nation-state, and the relationships among and between these variables.

In Chapter 8, Rokhshad Tavakoli provides a reflective account of her virtual journeys and how virtual tourism has represented an avenue to overcome Iranian women's barriers to travel. By embracing an 'auto-netnographic' approach, Rokhshad's work also paves the way for new ways of conducting and representing research on Asian genders in tourism.

Overall, with this book we hope to provide an overview of Asian gendered identities on holiday, as we believe that 'Asia' has been neglected by tourism scholars. While we appreciate that this collection is only a partial representation of the complexities of Asian genders travelling, we believe that the book will be of interest to tourism scholars focusing on gender, as it provides insights into this unknown universe.

References

Butler, G., Khoo-Lattimore, C. and Mura, P. (2014) Heritage tourism in Malaysia: Fostering a collective national identity in an ethnically diverse country. *Asia Pacific Journal of Tourism Research* 19 (2), 199–218. doi: 10.1080/10941665.2012.735682.

Henderson, K.A. and Gibson, H.J. (2013) An integrative review of women, gender, and leisure: Increasing complexities. *Journal of Leisure Research* 45 (2), 115–135.

Khoo-Lattimore, C. (2017) The ethics of excellence in tourism research: A reflexive analysis and implications for early career researchers. *Tourism Analysis* (forthcoming).

Kinnaird, V. and Hall, D. (1994) *Tourism: A Gender Analysis*. Chichester: Wiley.

Mura, P. and Pahlevan Sharif, S. (2015) The crisis of the 'crisis of representation' – Mapping qualitative tourism research in Southeast Asia. *Current Issues in Tourism* 18 (9), 828–844. doi: 10.1080/13683500.2015.1045459.

Oakley, A. (2006) Feminism isn't ready to be swept under the carpet. *Times Higher Education Supplement*, 3 March, pp. 18–19.

Pritchard, A., Morgan, N., Ateljevic, I. and Harris, C. (2007) *Tourism and Gender: Embodiment, Sensuality and Experience*. Wallingford: CABI.

Sinclair, M.T. (1997) *Gender, Work and Tourism*. London: Routledge.

Swain, M.M. and Momsen, J.H. (eds) (2002) *Gender/Tourism/Fun?* New York: Cognizant Communication.

Winter, T., Teo, P. and Chang, T.C. (2008) *Asia on Tour: Exploring the Rise of Asian Tourism*. Abington: Routledge.

World Tourism Organization (2015) Over 1.1 billion tourists travelled abroad in 2014. Press release online at http://media.unwto.org/press-release/2015-01-27/over-11-billion-tourists-travelled-abroad-2014 (accessed 27 April 2015).

2 Asian Gendered Identities in Tourism

Elaine Chiao Ling Yang and Paolo Mura

> *From culture to culture, the male–female distinction has been assigned meanings and significance that have implications for work, family, leisure, and ritual – virtually all aspects of social life.*
> (Lips, 2005: xiii)

Introduction

As a 'highly politically charged concept' (Bradley, 2007: 1), gender shapes many aspects of our lives (Burr, 1998), including our experiences as tourists (Swain, 1995). Kinnaird *et al.* (1994) point out that tourism is a phenomenon constructed within a gendered society, namely a space where gendered identities are formed, reproduced and contested. Likewise, Aitchison (2001: 134) argues that tourism should be conceived as 'a powerful cultural arena and process that both shapes and is shaped by gendered (re)presentations of places, people, nations and cultures'. Tourism scholars have acknowledged the importance of the gendered structures of power in shaping holiday experiences and tourists' patterns of behaviour. Indeed, the interest in the gendered nature of tourism has led to a proliferation of studies on gender in the last 30 years. While gender was rarely discussed within tourism academic circles until the mid-1970s, a plethora of studies on gender in tourism have been conducted since the 1980s (see Enloe, 1989; Garcia-Ramon *et al.*, 1995; Kariel & Kariel, 1982; Laver, 1987; Pritchard & Morgan, 2000; Wilson & Little, 2008). The emergence of gender research in tourism reflects many other social science disciplines, especially those focusing on human behaviour and social experience, where gender issues began to receive scholarly attention only after the second wave of the Western feminist movement, in the 1970s (Burgess-Proctor, 2006; Caterall & Maclaran, 2001).

Despite this, the limitations to essentialist and structuralist conceptualisations of gender, mainly based on the assumption that men and women are different due to biological factors (Grewal & Kaplan, 2006), have only recently been acknowledged. In this regard, only in the last 10 years have post-structuralist theories contemplating the existence of multiple 'genders' (rather than the parsimonious men/women simplistic dichotomy) become more prominent within the social sciences, including tourism studies. This has also led to the recognition that gendered identities in leisure and tourism experiences cannot be disentangled from other social constructs, such as ethnicity and socio-economic status.

Although postmodern discussions on gender have featured in other fields, little tourism research has engaged in the discourse. While these criticisms are being progressively addressed by tourism scholars, there are still conceptual issues that hamper an in-depth understanding of tourist gendered identities. A tourism issue that requires more attention is related to the idea that gendered identities are politically and socially constructed within specific socio-cultural contexts. As such, studies on gender conducted within certain societies may not be always applicable in different socio-cultural contexts. As most of the studies on gender and tourism have been conducted on Western societies (mainly by Western scholars), less is known about gendered tourist experiences in other contexts, such as Asia.

The challenges that gender scholars in tourism need to face mirror the obstacles that academicians in other fields of enquiry often encounter. In particular, calls for research to recognise the multiplicity of gender and to employ an intersectional approach to gender studies have also extended to geography (Valentine, 2007), criminology (Burgess-Proctor, 2006), the study of consumer behaviour (Caterall & Maclaran, 2001) and leisure studies (Henderson & Gibson, 2013). Broadbridge and Simpson (2011) discuss the 'precarious positioning' of gender in management research. More specifically, their work highlights the patriarchal narratives that are often reiterated to minimise gender-related issues. Among the linguistic strategies that tend to silence gendered problems, the idea that 'the problem of gender has been solved' seems to be predominant in managerial practices (Broadbridge & Simpson, 2011). This argument, which is often supported by statistical data showing that women are more visible in previously conceived 'forbidden' zones' at work or at leisure, is also reiterated within tourism academic circles. For instance, many tourism studies include gender as one of many variables to show that they have taken gender into account rather than genuinely focusing on the concept of gender itself or the gendered experience. Thus, as highlighted in Chapter 1, gender is often labelled as an 'old fashioned' topic (see Oakley, 2006). Likewise, some discourses propelled by tourism scholars seem to present similarities to management studies' arguments about the importance of valuing meritocracy irrespective of gender (see Broadbridge & Simpson, 2011). Although similar narratives find their place in other disciplines (Greene et al., 2003; Probert, 2005), we contend that tourist gendered identities need to be researched in greater detail to unveil the structures of power that activate these narratives. This is particularly true within the Asian context. While studies on gender in Asia do exist (see Hing *et al.*, 1984; Kelsky, 2001; Lebra & Paulson, 1980; Mernissi, 1987), there is a paucity of empirical material on Asian gendered identities on holiday, especially when masculinities are concerned.

Due to unprecedented rapid economic growth, the Asian tourism industry has flourished in the last 20 years. Within the region, China is widely recognised as the fastest-growing outbound market (World Tourism Organization, 2015) and many Southeast Asian countries have been identified as promising outbound markets (World Tourism Organization, 2013). Tourism researchers are aware of the significance of the Asian tourism market, as seen in the increasing number of publications on Asian tourists. Nevertheless, few studies have addressed gendered travel behaviour with deep reflection on Asian femininities and masculinities. Gender, in most cases, is treated as just one of many independent variables (see Huang, 2006; Kim *et al.*, 2013, 2015), representing the third phase – 'gender differences' – in Henderson and Gibson's (2013) gender scholarship framework. The resulting interpretations of gender differences in Asian tourist behaviour are often superficial and left unexplained. When gender is explored, the focus is exclusively on Asian women's experiences. Henderson and Gibson (2013) dub this phenomenon as the 'women only' phase of gender research.

Although there are a number of sociological publications on Asian masculinities (see Louie, 2015; Louie & Edwards, 1994; Taga, 2005), tourism scholars have not shown much interest in the relations between Asian men, masculinities and travel. Waitt and Markwell's (2006) comment on the Western-centric tendency in research on masculinities and tourism is still valid after a decade. For example, in Thurnell-Read and Casey's (2014) edited collection *Men, Masculinities, Travel and Tourism*, only two chapters out of 15 considered Asian men's experiences: Waitt and Markwell (2014) explored Indonesian men's experience and romance with Western/white tourists at a gay tourism destination in Bali; and Lin (2014) studied Taiwanese men's 'wife-finding tours' of Southeast Asia and mainland China. Apart from these, the voices of other forms of Asian masculinities remain silent in the contemporary tourism context.

By focusing on Asian gendered identities in tourism, this chapter attempts to address this gap in knowledge. First, the dominant ideologies and practices that have shaped gendered relations in Asia are presented. The multiple religious, cultural and political values that have contributed to produce Asian gendered identities over the centuries are briefly discussed. More specifically, the legacies of Confucianism and Islam in constructing male and female roles are examined in the next section of the chapter. Second, an analysis is conducted of the intricate system of contemporary socio-cultural trends, such as neoliberal globalisation, state deregulation and capitalism (which are continuously producing, deconstructing and reproducing Asian gendered identities). Thereafter, Asians' gendered identities during tourist experiences are discussed and critically analysed in the next section of the chapter.

In view of the dearth of studies on gender and tourism in Asia, this chapter pulls together the limited understandings of Asian gender(s) on holiday, mainly from women's perspective due to the lack of studies of Asian masculinities, with the aim of building a foundation for future exploration.

Gender in Asia

Asian values and gender relations

'Asia', a concept contemplated in the Greek literature as far back as the 5th century BC, is a term that was used to indicate the huge mass of hazy and mysterious land situated to the east of Europe (Knight, 2000). 'Asian' is therefore not an identity developed by *Asians* but a label put on them. Asian identities are socially constructed, invented and imagined by Westerners to describe what they believe exists in the East. Asia is constructed as a homogenised entity (Bui *et al.*, 2013) and 'Asianness' is oversimplified and overgeneralised. Yet, defining Asian values and their gender implications is a complicated task and the interpretation is subject to one's social situatedness (Knight, 2000). Although inconclusive, scholars have generally recognised the collectivist nature of Asians, whose identities and shared values have been based on an orderly society, social harmony, filial piety and respect for authority (Prideaux & Shiga, 2007; Sheridan, 1999).

There are many cultural ideologies and religions practised in Asia which have had an effect on the making of Asian gender(s). These include Confucianism in East Asia, Vietnam and other Chinese communities in Southeast Asia; Islam in South Indochina, Island Southeast Asia and West Asia; Theravada Buddhism in North Indochina; Hinduism in South Asia; and indigenous traditions across the region. This list is not exhaustive as there are many variations within the sub-regions. This chapter focuses on gender practices in East and Southeast Asia, and specific attention is given to social contexts under Confucian and Islamic influence. These two dominating ideologies influence the majority of the population in Asia. As far as gender is concerned, Confucianism and Islam have two things in common, which are the oppressed image of women and the dominant image of men. In general, Asian women in Confucian and Islamic societies are subscribed to a similar set of gender norms: submissive, domesticated and family oriented (Tang & Tang, 2001; Zhang & Hitchcock, 2014).

During the pre-modern period, the characteristic of femininity in Confucian societies involved the art of 'following' (Taga, 2005). In other words, women were taught to be submissive and to behave moderately.

Ideally, a virtuous wife should stay within the household and practise calligraphy, painting, zither and chess. These women were known as *guixiu* (which literally means women in the inner chamber) and had greater success in the marriage market (Ko, 1994; Qian, 2015). Contrastingly, the characteristic of masculinity was far more complicated. An ideal man should be able to present a balance between two opposite features: *wen* (mastery of arts and literature) and *wu* (command of martial arts) (Louie & Edwards, 1994). This gendered distinction was more common among the gentry. For the general public, mostly peasants during the agricultural age, gender relations were mediated by economic necessity, as women also partook in agricultural work rather than being totally free from economic production. However, Confucian teachings on gender distinction between outer (occupied by men) and inner (occupied by women) spaces were evident among the people and had been passed down for generations. For example, women were expected to bear all the caretaker responsibility within households. The gender division of inner–outer space was reinforced by the process of industrialisation, whose effect was twofold. On the one hand, with the disintegration of agricultural society, men became the primary breadwinners through their labour in factories and mines. One the other hand, even if women were hired as factory workers, they received lower pay, on the basis of their gender. Also, these working women still had to carry out their domestic responsibilities in addition to the long hours they spent in the factory. This resulted in a hegemonic form of masculinity which is still prevalent in many Asian societies. With the global promotion of gender equality in the past few decades, Asian women from (post)Confucian societies have achieved significant gender advancement in the education and economic spheres. However, a close investigation of women's travel behaviour shows that the shadow of Confucian values lingers (Guo, 2014; Zhang & Hitchcock, 2014).

Resembling the patriarchal Confucian societies, gender relations in Muslim societies have been condemned by scholars for subordinating women (Karim, 1995; Othman, 2006). In fact, some scholars contend that the gender hierarchy in the contemporary Muslim societies in Southeast Asia has widened as a result of radical Islamisation in the 1970s (Karim, 1995; Othman, 2006). In comparison with contemporary Muslim women, their female ancestors enjoyed a higher gender status in traditional society. Some anthropologists of gender opine that women in ancient Southeast Asia were probably less oppressed than those in Victorian society (Karim, 1995).

In the postcolonial nation-building period, two major transitions took place in Southeast Asia: democratisation and radical Islamisation (Derichs, 2013). As the goal and agenda of democracy were not gender sensitive, patriarchal authority infused Southeast Asian nations during the transition period. Moreover, the newly independent nations in Southeast Asia were searching for an identity in the face of globalisation, modernisation, Westernisation and secularisation (Knight, 2000). To safeguard national sovereignty and to reassert an 'authentic' cultural identity, Malaysia and Indonesia opted for Islamisation during the wave of global Islamic revivalism in the 1970s and 1980s (Othman, 2006; Schröter, 2013). An Arabic version of Islamic ideology was adopted by the male political elites who gained power during the transition process. The indigenous Malay cultural identity and its bilateral gender system were superseded by the patriarchal Arabised Islamic identity (Karim, 1995) – an identity which has been criticised for being discriminatory and oppressive to women (Othman, 2006). The transition in Southeast Asia therefore brought democracy and liberty to some people but authoritarian patriarchy and new forms of oppression to others, especially to Muslim women. Gender-discriminatory practices remain evident in the rights and status of Muslim women in family and society, including their limited rights relating to their body, sexuality and mobility (Othman, 2006). The influence of these societal and religious constraints on Muslim women's travel behaviour has been documented by Asbollah *et al.* (2013) and will be discussed in greater detail later in this chapter.

The traditional Asian gender structure is a complicated socio-cultural phenomenon whereby the power relations in the patriarchal political-economic structure and attitudes towards religious teachings and cultural values hold ultimate responsibility for the (in)equality between men and women (Jiang, 2009; Li, 2000; Taga, 2005; Valutanu, 2012). As mentioned, some Southeast Asian communities used to practise a bilateral gender system back in the agricultural era, although the hierarchical gender structure in religious practices was evident (Nwe, 2010; Van Esterick, 2000). The prevalence of patriarchal capitalism, nationalism and rapid industrialisation in the postcolonial era has transformed the traditional gender practices in the region. Using Thailand as an example, there are three sexes and four sexualities (Morris, 1994), shaped by indigenous gender traditions, Buddhism, Western influences through globalisation, and neo-colonialism in the form of tourism (Van Esterick, 2000).

In sum, Asian gender identities are essentially a social and cultural construction which continues to evolve. The making of Asian women and Asian men is subject to traditional values, religions and contemporary socio-cultural trends.

Gender and current socio-cultural trends in Asia

In general, current Asian identities have been shaped by an intricate system of 'contemporary' socio-cultural trends, including neoliberal globalisation, state deregulation, capitalism (and its massive consumptive practices), (post)modernity, middle-class values, urbanisation, changes in family size and composition, media oligopolies and transnational economies (Sen & Stivens, 1998). The word 'contemporary' here is compulsorily placed within inverted commas as socio-cultural phenomena, like globalisation and capitalism, are not new at all. Indeed, contacts between civilisations have existed since prehistoric times. Also, capitalist forces have appeared since the demise of feudalism. Yet, a number of factors, such as the technological advancements propelled by the Industrial Revolution, have led to an intensification and densification of these economic, social and cultural trends in (the) contemporary (world and) Asia (Loomba, 1998).

The socio-cultural phenomena that characterise Asian (post)modern societies have been discussed in the literature within the context of two major 'grand narratives'. The first tends to privilege optimistic conceptualisations of 'development' and places emphasis on socio-cultural progress, economic growth and political stability. 'Asian tigers', 'Asian dragons' and 'newly industrialised countries' (NICs) are often mentioned in the repertoire of terms employed to support this narrative of successful development in Asia. The second narrative is less optimistic, as it focuses on the issues arising from the achievement of 'development', such as the widening of economic inequalities, the increase in socio-cultural disparities and the increasing violation of human rights (Sen & Stivens, 1998). This narrative is more germane in portraying the abuses of power that have been perpetrated by certain Asian military regimes, as in Myanmar (Burma) and North Korea. This narrative does not hide the economic and social gap between the rich and the poor in those Asian economies perceived as 'more democratic'. Overall, these two narratives remind us that social and economic changes have occurred in a non-homogenous fashion in the different contexts constituting Asia. For example, capitalist societies, as in South Korea and Singapore, have followed a totally different pattern of development from other Asian contexts, such as Myanmar and North Korea. Also, within each society, variations between regions (e.g. between urban and rural areas) are still highly pronounced.

It is within this intricate scenario and its related hegemonic and subordinated narratives that the impact of new socio-cultural trends on Asian gendered identities and practices needs to be understood. While globalisation and the rise of a new middle class have partially contributed to challenge stereotypical, patriarchal images of femininity and masculinity, they have also helped to crystallise traditional, androcentric gender-based structures of power (Lindio-McGovern & Wallimann, 2009; Seguino & Grown, 2006). In reiterating how gendered inequalities and the predilection of the male gaze persist even behind economic growth, Hooper (1998) points out that Chinese women's (apparently 'liberating') consumptive patterns have tended to (re)produce subordinated images of women as 'sexual objects'. Indeed, as Sen and Stivens (1998: xi) put it, 'the same clothes and cosmetics that liberated the Chinese woman's body from the drab communist uniform also reshaped the body as an object of display, selling everything from calendars to computers'. Likewise, Purkayastha and Majumdar (2009) argue that neoliberal globalisation has contributed in part to fill 'gendered gaps'; yet, it has also intensified sex trafficking and the commodification of Asian women within the region.

Current socio-cultural trends have also problematised Asian masculine identities and practices (Kimmel *et al.*, 2005). In Taiwan, low-skilled and low-income men find themselves facing a dilemma in fulfilling the expectations of hegemonic masculinity (Connell, 2005; Lin, 2014). In the patriarchal heterosexual marriage system, men are expected to have a higher social position than women. As Taiwanese women's social position has greatly improved with their access to higher education and professional careers, men of lower social status face challenges in finding the 'ideal' wife and are falling into a marginalised masculinity (Connell, 2015). To exert their maleness, many turn to foreign brides from less developed societies, such as Southeast Asia and rural areas of China (Lin, 2014). In Japan, recent global trends, supported by governmental policies aimed at promoting gender equality, have attempted to erode the 'myth' of hegemonic masculinity. Yet, 'salaryman' culture, mainly grounded on the man-breadwinner/woman-housewife patriarchal dichotomy, still plays a major role in the construction of 'maleness' (Taga, 2005). In this respect, Taga (2005) unveils the psychological difficulties of 'becoming a man' in Japan, as males need to constantly reconcile what they perceive as two conflicting roles, namely hegemonic 'salaryman' and subordinated 'family man'.

The complexities behind the formation and acquisition of Asian masculine identities in current globalised contexts are also discussed by Balaji (2011: 187), who observes that 'despite the globalisation of media and the supposed celebration of multiculturalism, representations of Asian masculinity in film and television have, for the most part, remained Othered'. In other words, while within patriarchal paradigms Asian men and women are conceived as hegemonic and subordinated cohorts respectively, post-structuralist and postcolonial theories emphasise the subordinated role of Asian masculinities and the ideological supremacy of the 'Western male' in the global scenario (Bhabha, 1994). Importantly, the social fabrication of marginal Asian masculinities plays a crucial role in the politics of gendered representation, which tends to privilege the dominant 'maleness' of Western men (Nakayama, 1994).

This complex system of socio-cultural forces characterising (post)modernity has also reshaped 'malestream' perceptions concerning the meaning of 'public' and 'private' spheres. In this regard, the picture of emancipated, urban Asian women emerging after the Second World War symbolises a shift of power in traditional Confucian ideologies, which situate males as dominant figures in public spaces and females as 'followers' in domestic realms (Rosaldo, 1974; Taga, 2005). However, the fragility of these apparent changes should not be overlooked, as variations still exist between urban and rural Asian women and men. Moreover, these changes need to be framed within the context of existing ethnic and class inequalities, which in turn shape gendered identities and contribute to produce hegemonic and marginalised masculinities and femininities (Lindio-McGovern & Wallimann, 2009; McClintock, 1995).

In other words, Asian gendered identities cannot transcend the paradoxes of (post)modernity, namely the myriad of incongruences and tensions between 'global' and 'local' forces. It is within these paradoxes that Asian gendered identities are performed, accepted, questioned, challenged and reinvented. It is within this multifaceted political and socio-cultural scenario that the intricate universe of masculine and feminine identities comes to life in Asia and is reproduced in tourism settings.

Asian Holidays

East Asia and (post)Confucian societies

Under the neoliberal globalisation framework, Chinese women today have achieved unprecedented economic independence, with improved access to education and employment opportunities. They are recognised as lavish spenders, with a predilection for shopping, and they prefer independent travel over packaged tours (Li et al., 2011). For Chinese women, the motivations to travel are to enhance both knowledge and social status (Li et al., 2011), as well as to relax and pamper themselves (Zhang & Hitchcock, 2014). Tourism provides Chinese women a space outside their everyday lives, or, to use Foucault's (1990) term, a *heterotopia*, where they can reconstruct their gender identity and gain a sense of self-worth (Zhang & Hitchcock, 2014). Nevertheless, studies have highlighted the ambivalent travel attitude and gender identity of Chinese women (Guo, 2014; Zhang & Hitchcock, 2014). For instance, some Chinese tourists reported concerns about their familial obligations at home while they were away on holiday (Zhang & Hitchcock, 2014). Contrastingly, professional, career-oriented Chinese women regard family holidays as opportunities in which to fulfil their traditional gender roles as dutiful wives, mothers and daughters that they are unable to perform in their hectic daily lives (Zhang & Hitchcock, 2014). The contradicting gender ideologies and practices are manifestations of the perpetuation of Confucian traditions in modernised China (Guo, 2014). This paradoxical gender identity is reflected in the polarised travel behaviour of Chinese women. For instance, in Huang's (2006) study on the travel behaviour of Chinese international students, it was found that young Chinese women outnumbered men in the most expensive categories of accommodation (e.g. luxury hotels) and the cheapest categories (e.g. backpacker hostels).

In the less developed areas of China, women may not be as fortunate as the urban professional Chinese women who have the capacity to travel at freewill. There is another form of travel taking place in this part of the world and in many Southeast Asian countries – the international marriage tour. Lin (2014) provides important perspectives on the construction and manipulation of masculinity in Taiwanese men's 'wife-finding tours' and the commodification of Asian women of low social status. As mentioned at the beginning of this chapter, little research has discussed Asian men's travel experiences from a gender perspective. Lin's (2014) work advances our understanding concerning how the ideal and the actual masculinities shape Taiwanese men's travel behaviour, although her study was based on a niche tourism market and on observations and interviews with the foreign wives rather than the men themselves.

As a result of rapid internationalisation in the 1980s, Japanese women began to travel abroad (Lang *et al.*, 1994); they are essentially therefore the vanguards of Asian female travellers. In the 1990s, Japanese female tourists/travellers were reported to prefer group travel and packaged tours (Cai & Combrink, 2000; Lang *et al.*, 1994). The majority of these Japanese women were either homemakers or clerical officers, and their main travel motivations were to escape, relax and pursue lifelong learning (Cai & Combrink, 2000). Research conducted in the new century began to illustrate a different landscape: contemporary Japanese female tourists are recognised as unmarried, career-minded working women who have disposable incomes for luxury shopping and overseas travel (Toyota, 2006). Hashimoto (2000) characterised young Japanese women travellers as adventurous and independent people who prefer individual-based travel and who have a predilection for holiday romance. Moreover, it is evident that feminist ideology has gained a foothold among Japanese women (Hashimoto, 2000). While conforming to the patriarchal gender norms that require them to be submissive and subordinate, especially after marriage, young single Japanese women resist gender oppression in alternative ways, such as travelling overseas and pursuing holiday romances (Hashimoto, 2000; Toyota, 2006).

Since the removal in the late 1980s of a curb on overseas travel (McGahey, 1991), the South Korean outbound travel market has grown drastically, reinforced by rapid economic growth and Korean globalisation policy (Bui *et al.*, 2013). According to prior research on Asian independent travellers in general, South Korean tourists are young and generally university students from relatively affluent families (Bui *et al.*, 2013), and they make up a significant portion of the working holiday market in Australia (Nagai *et al.*, 2014). However, across the mainstream English-language tourism journals, only a handful of articles have considered Korean tourists with attention to gender. For instance, Kim *et al.* (2011) measured the effect of gender on the travel decision-making process; and Kim *et al.* (2013) examined the impact of gender on online tourism shopping. While both these quantitative studies reported statistically significant gender differences, the authors did not expound on them.

Southeast Asia and Islamic societies

Southeast Asia has recently emerged as an important source market for intra-regional and Australian tourism (Reisinger & Turner, 2002; World Tourism Organization, 2013). Tourists from this region tend to be young and well educated, which is a manifestation of gentrification due to the rapid economic growth within the region since the 1990s (Bui *et al.*, 2013; Yang *et al.*, 2015). Despite its growing significance in the outbound travel market, the tourism literature tends to approach Southeast Asia from a production perspective as far as gender is concerned. Gender-tourism studies of this region tend to focus on female and transgender sex workers (Bernstein & Shih, 2014; Keller, 2014; Ocha & Earth, 2013) and the gendered division of labour in community-based tourism (Phommavong & Sörensson, 2012; Tran & Walter, 2014). Few studies have considered gender from a consumption angle, and the exceptions have looked at the experiences mainly of Southeast Asian women (see Asbollah *et al.*, 2013; Chan, 2007). Resonating with our observation earlier, there is clearly a dearth of research concerning the relations between Southeast Asian men, masculinities and travel. Waitt and Markwell's (2014) study is one of the very few to investigate Southeast Asian men in a tourism context using a gender approach. Their work was on gay Indonesian men who migrated to Bali and their romance and/or sexual relationships with tourists.

Asbollah *et al.* (2013) provide seminal insights into the understanding of Southeast Asian female travel experiences in an Islamic context. The authors studied the travel behaviour and motivation of Malay Muslim women and unveiled the 'cultural bubble' (Asbollah *et al.*, 2013: 687) that constrains Muslim women's travel behaviour. This cultural bubble encompasses both socially constructed gender roles (e.g. familial obligations and concerns about safety) and Islamic practices (e.g. halal food, prayer and Islamic dress code). Although Asbollah *et al.* (2013) discuss the influence of religion and culture on Muslim women's holiday experiences, the authors conjecture that the forces of modernisation and globalisation are likely to infuse the 'cultural bubble', leading Asian Muslim women to seek more individualistic and independent travel experiences. Kim *et al.* (2015) found that Asian Muslim women have greater preference than men for packaged tours and fashion/jewellery shopping, while the men prefer independent forms of travel. The authors simply regard this statistical difference as 'understandable because females tend to choose safer, more developed, or urban destinations rather than wild, isolated, or adventure-filled settings' (Kim *et al.*, 2015: 15) without explaining why it is 'understandable' and how femininities and masculinities work in the contemporary Asian context. This interpretation reminds us that post-essentialist interpretations of gender are relatively neglected by Asian scholars, as stereotypical images of 'adventurous men' and 'fearful women' are still contemplated within the tourism literature.

As tourism scholars are 'socialised' within gendered societies and gendered academic contexts, it is not surprising that the complexity of Asian genders (in terms of multifaceted and diverse masculinities and femininities) has not received much attention within Asian academic circles.

Conclusion

This chapter has focused on Asian gendered identities in tourism. It has presented and discussed the historical, religious, social and political events that have shaped (and still shape) gender relations in Asia and, subsequently, Asians' tourism experiences. Despite referring to 'Asia' and 'Asians' as homogenous social constructs, this work emphasises the diversity of the religious, cultural, social, economic and political values that characterise the Asian continent. For instance, Asians, including Confucian and Islamic societies, share an image of subordinate women, but the meanings of femininities and masculinities vary across different social and cultural contexts and across the spectrum of heteronormativity. These ideological frameworks have deeply influenced the ways in which Asians have approached tourism. As presented earlier, professional, working Chinese women see family holidays as an opportunity to fulfil their filial and familial obligations, while young, single Japanese women see independent travel or even holiday romance as a way to resist traditional gender norms, which they are nonetheless likely to embrace after getting married. For Taiwanese men of low social status, certain types of travel (e.g. 'wife-finding tours') empower them with a sense of 'maleness' or hegemonic masculinity. For Muslim women, religious practices affect their travel behaviour and choice of destination. Some examples include the availability of halal food and the use of prayer rooms. But religion does not refrain some Muslim men from pursuing same-sex romance with tourists, although they risk being marginalised in the society they belong to. As such, conceptualisations of 'Asia' and 'Asianness' should not overlook the fact that Asian identities and the gendered patterns of travel behaviour differ considerably among (and within) the various Asian countries. Rather, within the context of this chapter the terms 'Asia' and 'Asian' are employed to indicate broad categories which encompass a myriad of socially and politically produced identities.

Importantly, the existence of multiple identities within the region translates into a complex interplay of gender identities and relations. As Asian identities are multiple and complicated, so are Asian gendered identities on holiday. Furthermore, Asian male and female travelling experiences cannot be understood without taking this complex scenario into consideration. Unfortunately, this chapter underlines that the complexity of Asian gendered identities on holiday has not been properly addressed by tourism scholars. Indeed, studies on Asian genders in tourism are limited and fragmented.

Moreover, the paucity of studies on Asian masculinities on holiday hampers our understanding of gender and tourism in Asia.

Overall, the studies presented in this chapter show that tourism provides a context in which Asian gendered identities are formed, reproduced, represented and contested. However, little is known about the socio-cultural and political processes that influence (and are influenced by) the politics of gender identity formation during Asian travelling experiences. In view of these considerations, this chapter calls for more research on Asian genders on holiday. Indeed, new studies are necessary to unveil the global and local forces that shape Asian gendered identities in specific tourism contexts. Importantly, not only Western scholars but also Asian academicians should be actively involved in the production of scholarly work on Asian genders and tourism. This will provide multiple perspectives on Asian identities, which in turn will deepen our understanding of gender relations and cast more light on how Asian masculinities and femininities 'work' on holiday.

References

Aitchison, C. (2001) Theorizing other discourses of tourism, gender and culture: Can the subaltern speak (in tourism)? *Tourist Studies* 1 (2), 133–147. doi: 10.1177/146879760100100202.

Asbollah, A.Z.B., Lade, C. and Michael, E. (2013) The tourist's gaze: From the perspective of a Muslim woman. *Tourism Analysis* 18 (6), 677–690. doi: 10.3727/108354213X138 24558188703.

Balaji, M. (2011) Beyond Jackie Chan. In R.L. Jackson II and M. Balaji (eds) *Global Masculinities and Manhood* (pp. 186–201). Champaign, IL: University of Illinois Press.

Bernstein, E. and Shih, E. (2014) The erotics of authenticity: Sex trafficking and 'reality tourism' in Thailand. *Social Politics: International Studies in Gender, State and Society* 21 (3), 430–460. doi: 10.1093/sp/jxu022.

Bhabha, H. (1994) *The Location of Culture*. New York: Routledge.

Bradley, H. (2007) *Gender*. Cambridge: Polity Press.

Broadbridge, A. and Simpson, R. (2011) 25 years on: Reflecting on the past and looking to the future in gender and management research. *British Journal of Management* 22 (3), 470–483. doi: 10.1111/j.1467-8551.2011.00758.x.

Bui, H.T., Wilkins, H.C. and Lee, Y.-S. (2013) The 'imagined West' of young independent travellers from Asia. *Annals of Leisure Research* 16 (2), 130–148. doi: 10.1080/11745398.2013.791227.

Burgess-Proctor, A. (2006) Intersections of race, class, gender, and crime: Future directions for feminist criminology. *Feminist Criminology* 1 (1), 27–47. doi: 10.1177/1557085105282899.

Burr, V. (1998) *Gender and Social Psychology*. London: Routledge.

Cai, L.A. and Combrink, T.E. (2000) Japanese female travelers – A unique outbound market. *Asia Pacific Journal of Tourism Research* 5 (1), 16–24. doi: 10.1080/10941660008722055.

Caterall, M.A. and Maclaran, P.B. (2001) Gender perspectives in consumer behaviour: An overview and future directions. *Marketing Review* 2 (4), 405–425. doi: 10.1362/1469347012863853.

Chan, B. (2007) Film-induced tourism in Asia: A case study of Korean television drama and female viewers' motivation to visit Korea. *Tourism Culture and Communication* 7 (3), 207–224. doi: 10.3727/ 109830407782212510.

Connell, R.W. (2005) *Masculinities*. London: Polity Press.
Derichs, C. (2013) Gender and transition in Southeast Asia: Conceptual travel? *Asia Europe Journal* 11 (2), 113–127. doi: 10.1007/s10308-013-0342-x.
Enloe, C. (1989) *Bananas, Beaches and Bases: Making Feminist Sense of International Politics*. London: Pandora.
Foucault, M. (1990) *The History of Sexuality*. New York: Vintage Books.
Garcia-Ramon, M.D., Canoves, G. and Valdovinos, N. (1995) Farm tourism, gender and the environment in Spain. *Annals of Tourism Research* 22 (2), 267–282.
Greene, P.G., Hart, M.M., Gatewood, E.J., Brush, C.G. and Carter, N.M. (2003) Women entrepreneurs: Moving front and center. An overview of research and theory. *Coleman White Paper Series* 3, 1–47.
Grewal, I. and Kaplan, C. (2006) *An Introduction to Women's Studies: Gender in a Transnational World*. New York: McGraw Hill.
Guo, Y. (2014) Chinese women and travel: Historical and contemporary experiences. *Annals of Tourism Research* 46, 179–181. doi: 10.1016/j.annals.2014.02.004.
Hashimoto, A. (2000) Young Japanese female tourists: An in-depth understanding of a market segment. *Current Issues in Tourism* 3 (1), 35–50. doi: 10.1080/13683500008667865.
Henderson, K.A. and Gibson, H.J. (2013) An integrative review of women, gender, and leisure: Increasing complexities. *Journal of Leisure Research* 45 (2), 115–135.
Hing, A.Y., Karim, N.S. and Talib, R. (1984) *Women in Malaysia*. Petaling Jaya: Pelanduk.
Hooper, B. (1998) 'Flower vase and housewife': Women and consumerism in post-Mao China. In K. Sen and M. Stivens (eds) *Gender and Power in Affluent Asia* (pp. 167–193). New York: Routledge.
Huang, R. (2006) A study of gender differences: The travel behaviour of Chinese international students studying in the UK. *Tourism* 54 (1), 63–69.
Jiang, X. (2009) Confucianism, women, and social contexts. *Journal of Chinese Philosophy* 36 (2), 228–242. doi: 10.1111/j.1540-6253.2009.01516.x.
Kariel, H.G. and Kariel, P.E. (1982) Socio-cultural impacts of tourism: An example from the Austrian Alps. *Geografiska Annaler, Series B* 64, 1–16.
Karim, W.J. (ed.) (1995) *'Male' and 'Female' in Developing Southeast Asia*. Oxford: Berg.
Keller, M. (2014) *An Analysis on Sex Work and Sex Tourism in Myanmar*. Chiang Mai: Tourism Transparency.
Kelsky, K. (2001) *Women on the Verge: Japanese Women, Western Dreams*. Durham, NC: Duke University Press.
Kim, M.-J., Lee, M.J., Lee, C.-K. and Song, H.-J. (2011) Does gender affect Korean tourists' overseas travel? Applying the model of goal-directed behavior. *Asia Pacific Journal of Tourism Research* 17 (5), 509–533. doi: 10.1080/10941665.2011.627355.
Kim, M.-J., Lee, C.-K. and Chung, N. (2013) Investigating the role of trust and gender in online tourism shopping in South Korea. *Journal of Hospitality and Tourism Research* 37 (3), 377–401. doi: 10.1177/1096348012436377.
Kim, S., Im, H.H. and King, B.E. (2015) Muslim travelers in Asia: The destination preferences and brand perceptions of Malaysian tourists. *Journal of Vacation Marketing* 21 (1), 3–21. doi:10.1177/ 1356766714549648.
Kimmel, M., Hearn J. and Connell, R.W. (2005) *Handbook on Studies on Men and Masculinities*. Thousand Oaks, CA: Sage.
Kinnaird, V., Kothari, U. and Hall, D. (1994) Tourism: Gender perspectives. In V. Kinnaird and D. Hall (eds) *Tourism – A Gender Analysis* (pp. 1–34). Chichester: Wiley.
Knight, N. (2000) *Thinking About Asia: An Australian Introduction to East and Southeast Asia*. Hindmarsh: Crawford House.
Ko, D. (1994) *Teachers of the Inner Chambers: Women and Culture in Seventeenth-Century China*. Stanford, CA: Stanford University Press.

Lang, C.-T., O'Leary, D.J.T. and Morrison, A.M. (1994) Activity segmentation of Japanese female overseas travelers. *Journal of Travel and Tourism Marketing* 2 (4), 1–22. doi: 10.1300/ J073v02n04_01.
Laver, A. (1987) Spanish tourism migrants: The case of Lloret de Mar. *Annals of Tourism Research* 14 (4), 449–470.
Lebra, J. and Paulson, J. (1980) *Chinese Women in Southeast Asia*. Singapore: Times Books International.
Li, C. (ed.) (2000) *The Sage and the Second Sex: Confucianism, Ethics, and Gender*. Chicago, IL: Open Court.
Li, M., Wen, T. and Leung, A. (2011) An exploratory study of the travel motivation of Chinese female outbound tourists. *Journal of China Tourism Research* 7 (4), 411–424. doi: 10.1080/ 19388160 .2011.627020.
Lin, C.-Y. (2014) Taiwanese men's wife-finding tours in Southeast Asian countries and China. In T. Thurnell-Read and M. Casey (eds) *Men, Masculinities, Travel and Tourism* (pp. 141–155). Basingstoke: Palgrave Macmillan.
Lindio-McGovern, L. and Wallimann, I. (2009) *Globalization and Third World Women: Exploitation, Coping and Resistance*. Farnham: Ashgate Publishing.
Lips, H.M. (2005) *Sex and Gender – An Introduction* (5th edn.). New York: McGraw-Hill.
Loomba, A. (1998) *Colonialism/Postcolonialism*. London: Routledge.
Louie, K. (2015) *Chiniese Masculinities in a Globalizing World*. New York: Routledge.
Louie, K. and Edwards, L. (1994) Chinese masculinity: Theorizing wen and wu. *East Asian History* 8, 135–148.
McClintock, A. (1995) *Imperial Leather: Race, Gender and Sexuality in the Colonial Context*. London: Routledge.
McGahey, S. (1991) South Korea outbound. *Travel and Tourism Analyst* 6, 45–62.
Mernissi, F. (1987) *Beyond the Veil: Male–Female Dynamics in Modern Muslim Society* (revised edn). Bloomington, IN: Indiana University Press.
Morris, R.C. (1994) Three sexes and four sexualities: Redressing the discourses on gender and sexuality in contemporary Thailand. *Positions* 2 (1), 15–43. doi: 10.1215/10679847-2-1-15.
Nagai, H., Benckendorff, P. and Tkaczynski, A. (2014) Exploring travel risk perceptions among Asian working holiday makers in Australia: A qualitative approach. In P.M. Chien (ed.) *CAUTHE 2014. Tourism and Hospitality in the Contemporary World: Trends, Changes and Complexity* (pp. 429–443). Brisbane: Council of Australasian Tourism and Hospitality Educators.
Nakayama, T.K. (1994) Show/down time: 'Race,' gender, sexuality, and popular cult. *Critical Studies in Mass Communication* 11, 162–178.
Nwe, A. (2010) Gender hierarchy in Myanmar. *CTC Bulletin* 26 (1), 131–139.
Ocha, W. and Earth, B. (2013) Identity diversification among transgender sex workers in Thailand's sex tourism industry. *Sexualities* 16 (1–2), 195–216. doi: 10.1177/1363460712471117.
Othman, N. (2006) Muslim women and the challenge of Islamic fundamentalism/extremism: An overview of Southeast Asian Muslim women's struggle for human rights and gender equality. *Women's Studies International Forum* 29 (4), 339–353. doi: 10.1016/j.wsif.2006.05.008.
Phommavong, S. and Sörensson, E. (2012) Ethnic tourism in Lao PDR: Gendered divisions of labour in community-based tourism for poverty reduction. *Current Issues in Tourism* 17 (4), 350–362. doi: 10.1080/13683500.2012.721758.
Prideaux, B. and Shiga, H. (2007) Japanese backpacking: The emergence of a new market sector – A Queensland case study. *Tourism Review International* 11 (1), 45–56. doi: 10.3727/ 1544272077 84771879.
Pritchard, A. and Morgan, N.J. (2000) Privileging the male gaze – Gendered tourism landscapes. *Annals of Tourism Research* 27 (4), 884–905.

Pritchard, A., Morgan, N., Ateljevic, I. and Harris, C. (2007) *Tourism and Gender: Embodiment, Sensuality and Experience*. Wallingford: CABI.
Probert, B. (2005) 'I just couldn't fit it in': Gender and unequal outcomes in academic careers. *Gender, Work and Organization* 12 (1), 50–72. doi: 10.1111/j.1468-0432.2005.00262.x.
Purkayastha, B. and Majumdar, S. (2009) Globalization and the sexual commodification of women. In L. Lindio-McGovern and I. Wallimann (eds) *Globalization and Third World Women: Exploitation, Coping and Resistance*. Farnham: Ashgate Publishing.
Qian, N. (2015) *Politics, Poetics, and Gender in Late Qing China: Xue Shaoui and the Era of Reform*. Stanford, CA: Stanford University Press.
Oakley, A. (2006) Feminism isn't ready to be swept under the carpet. *Times Higher Education Supplement*, 3 March, pp. 18–19.
Reisinger, Y. and Turner, L.W. (2002) Cultural differences between Asian tourist markets and Australian hosts, part 1. *Journal of Travel Research* 40 (3), 295–315. doi: 10.1177/004728750204000308.
Rosaldo, M.Z. (1974) Woman, culture, and society: A theoretical overview. In M.Z. Rosaldo and L. Lamphere (eds) *Woman, Culture and Society* (pp. 17–42). Standford, CA: Stanford University Press.
Schröter, S. (ed.) (2013) *Gender and Islam in Southeast Asia: Women's Rights Movements, Religious Resurgence and Local Traditions*. Leiden: Brill.
Seguino, S. and Grown, C. (2006) Gender equity and globalization: Macroeconomic policy for developing countries. *Journal of International Development* 18, 1–24.
Sen, K. and Stivens, M. (1998) *Gender and Power in Affluent Asia*. New York: Routledge.
Sheridan, G. (1999) *Asian Values Western Dreams*. St Leonards: Allen & Unwin.
Swain, M.B. (1995) Gender in tourism. *Annals of Tourism Research* 22 (2), 247–266.
Taga, F. (2005) East Asian masculinities. In M.S. Kimmel, J. Hearn and R.W. Connell (eds) *Handbook of Studies on Men and Masculinities*. Thousand Oaks, CA: Sage.
Tang, T.N. and Tang, C.S. (2001) Gender role internalization, multiple roles, and Chinese women's mental health. *Psychology of Women Quarterly* 25 (3), 181–196. doi: 10.1111/1471-6402.00020.
Thurnell-Read, T. and Casey, M. (eds) (2014) *Men, Masculinities, Travel and Tourism*. Basingstoke: Palgrave Macmillan.
Toyota, M. (2006) Consuming images: Young female Japanese tourists in Bali, Indonesia. In K. Meethan, A. Anderson and S. Miles (eds) *Tourism Consumption and Representation: Narratives of Place and Self* (pp. 158–177). Cambridge, MA: CABI.
Tran, L. and Walter, P. (2014) Ecotourism, gender and development in northern Vietnam. *Annals of Tourism Research* 44, 116–130. doi: 10.1016/j.annals.2013.09.005.
Valentine, G. (2007) Theorizing and researching intersectionality: A challenge for feminist geography. *The Professional Geographer* 59 (1), 10–21. doi: 10.1111/j.1467-9272.2007.00587.x.
Valutanu, L.I. (2012) Confucius and feminism. *Journal of Research in Gender Studies* 2 (1), 132–140.
Van Esterick, P. (2000) *Materializing Thailand*. Oxford: Berg.
Waitt, G. and Markwell, K. (2006) *Gay Tourism: Culture and Context*. New York: Haworth Press.
Waitt, G. and Markwell, K. (2014) 'I don't want to think I am a prostitute': Embodied geographies of men, masculinities and clubbing in Seminyak, Bali, Indonesia. In T. Thurnell-Read and M. Casey (eds) *Men, Masculinities, Travel and Tourism* (pp. 104–119). Basingstoke: Palgrave Macmillan.
Wilson, E. and Little, D.E. (2008) The solo female travel experience: Exploring the 'geography of women's fear'. *Current Issues in Tourism* 11 (2), 167–186.
World Tourism Organization (2013) UNWTO/Tourism Australia report highlights the potential of South-East Asian outbound tourism. Press release online at http://media.

unwto.org/press-release/2013-04-29/unwtotourism-australia-report-highlights-potential-south-east-asian-outboun (accessed May 2016).

World Tourism Organization (2015) Over 1.1 billion tourists travelled abroad in 2014. Press release online at http://media.unwto.org/press-release/2015-01-27/over-11-billion-tourists-travelled-abroad-2014 (accessed May 2016).

Yang, E.C.L., Sharif, S.P. and Khoo-Lattimore, C. (2015) Tourists' risk perception of risky destinations: The case of Sabah's eastern coast. *Tourism and Hospitality Research*. Advance online publication. doi: 10.1177/1467358415576085.

Zhang, Y. and Hitchcock, M.J. (2014) The Chinese female tourist gaze: A netnography of young women's blogs on Macao. *Current Issues in Tourism*. Advance online publication. doi: 10.1080/13683500.2014.904845.

3 'Doing' Tourism Gender Research in Asia: An Analysis of Authorship, Research Topic and Methodology

Elaine Chiao Ling Yang and
Rokhshad Tavakoli

Introduction

In recognition of the economic impact of the tourism industry, tourism and hospitality education in Asia has expanded rapidly over the past decade (Hsu, 2015). However, the development of tourism and tourism education is inconsistent within the region. For example, in countries subject to terrorism and political instability (e.g. in the Middle East), tourist arrivals have dropped off markedly and some areas have seen stagnant development or even the closure of tourism institutions. We know little about tourists coming from and travelling to the Middle East. In East and Southeast Asia, where tourism education prospers, many universities have adopted an internationalisation approach, such as adopting curricula from Western universities and offering courses in English (Hsu, 2015; Mok, 2007), attracting both female and male students and academics from the region and the West. This provides Asians, especially Asian women who had limited access to higher education until recently, with the opportunity to improve their English-language proficiency, which empowers them to engage in international scholarly discourse by publishing papers in English-language journals. Although the debate on the impact of international (English-language) journals versus local publications remains unresolved (Mok, 2007), based on our observation, and supported by Henderson and Gibson (2013), English-language publications on Asians, gender and tourism by Asian scholars have begun to emerge in tourism and leisure studies.

While tourism research concerning Asians and gender has become more prevalent in the international scholarly literature, we still know very little about Asian women and men consuming tourism spaces and products. This dearth of research (i.e. gendered tourism studies in Asia) is highlighted in Chapters 1 and 2, so here we focus on how the handful of available studies have approached Asian gender and tourism. More specifically, this chapter provides an analysis of the authorship, common research topics and methodology within these papers. The discussion of authorship addresses power relations in the production of knowledge, such as who produces knowledge for whom and from whose perspective. By looking at common topics, we can identify the current research trends and gaps. Analysis of the methodologies allows us to understand how Asians' travel experience has been studied thus far and what epistemological stances have been embraced by tourism researchers.

Gender Research in Tourism

'Tourism is a constellation of human practices, behaviours and activities, which are gendered in their construction, presentation and consumption' (Figueroa-Domecq *et al.*, 2015: 87). Scholars have cautioned that women and men experience tourism differently, both as tourists and as tourism providers (Pritchard *et al.*, 2007; Swain, 1995). Nevertheless, the existing corpus of tourism research appears to be highly gender blind. The first tourism article to consider gender or women's travel experience was by Smith (1979). Since then, the number of tourism gender studies has increased gradually but it remains a marginalised area (Figueroa-Domecq *et al.*, 2015). For example, studies of gender account for only one-tenth of the overall research within the tourism sub-fields of destination and community (Figueroa-Domecq *et al.*, 2015).

There are two possible explanations for the slow progress of gender research in tourism. First of all, tourism is dominated by business-oriented research, where scientific and (post)positivistic research is privileged (Pritchard *et al.*, 2007). Although tourism social science and critical tourism studies have gain a foothold in the field, many established scholars still attest the hegemonic status of business or management research in tourism, especially in institutions where tourism is operated through business schools (Tribe, 2010). This is especially true in Asia, where the economic and marketing aspects of tourism have received more attention, and tourism as an extension of social and cultural phenomena has been neglected. Second, gender research in tourism has been eclipsed by postmodernism (Pritchard *et al.*, 2007). In postmodernist discourse, gender is deconstructed and gender research is disintegrated before it is able to form a sub-field in tourism. As a consequence, feminist/gender research, which is value-laden, embodied and voiced, is marginalised.

Within the limited gender research in tourism, most studies have been conducted by Western scholars (Figueroa-Domecq *et al.*, 2015; Henderson & Gibson, 2013; Henderson & Hickerson, 2007). As gender is subject to cultural interpretations, findings from the West cannot be applied indiscriminately in an Asian context. However, a review by Henderson and Gibson (2013) noted the growing presence of leisure gender research conducted by Asian scholars, although the number of studies remains small. Figueroa-Domecq et al. (2015) reported a similar trend but further revealed that although few studies were by Asian scholars, 20.8% of tourism gender research fieldworks were conducted in Asia by Western scholars. The authors did not detail whether these studies conducted in Asia concerned Asian or Western tourists. We argue that even if Asians were studied, Western scholars might not be able to fully grasp the subtle gender norms and gender performances shaped by Asian ideologies. Hence, we ask the following questions: Whose perspective (Western or Asian scholars, male or female) has tourism gender research in Asia concerned? What and how do we know about the travel experience of Asian women and men? To answer these questions, we examine the tourism research concerning Asian gender, focusing on authorship, research topic and methodology.

'Doing' Gender Research in Tourism

Figueroa-Domecq et al. (2015) conducted a bibliometric analysis of tourism gender research that examined both tourism-related journals and journals from other disciplines (e.g. gender/women's studies, geography, and environmental studies). Their findings revealed the dominant status of quantitative methods in researching gendered tourist behaviour. Most of the quantitative papers were published in tourism-related journals. There were a considerable number of qualitative studies on gender and tourism, and a significant proportion of those were published in gender-related journals which embrace interpretive and critical approaches. This finding substantiates the (post)positivistic dominance of epistemology in tourism research, especially in tourism-related journals. Figueroa-Domecq et al. (2015), however, do not perceive qualitative research as the solution to feminist or gender questions in tourism, as the authors believe that the choice of methodology should depend on the nature of the questions to be answered in each individual study. Rather, Figueroa-Domecq et al. (2015) see mixed methods and multidisciplinary methods as the approaches more likely to be beneficial in broadening and deepening existing understanding of gender in tourism.

On the other hand, Henderson and Gibson (2013), who had earlier reviewed gender research in leisure studies, found that interpretative qualitative methods such as in-depth interviews have continued to be advocated by leisure/gender researchers because qualitative tools are instrumental in giving individuals voices and in explaining leisure experiences. They also observe the growing presence of reflexive approaches such as autoethnography and memory work. Only 20% of the papers in their review utilised quantitative methods.

The discrepancy between the two studies, Henderson and Gibson (2013) and Figueroa-Domecq *et al.* (2015), can be attributed to the inherent nature of the two sister fields. Leisure and tourism are closely related but they are different in terms of the research agenda and focus. In particular, leisure research is concerned with enhancing life, while tourism research focuses on business and management implications (Wilson, 2004).

'Doing' Tourism Research in Asia

Mura and Sharif (2015) brought to light the landscape of tourism research in Southeast Asia by revealing how tourism knowledge is produced in post-colonised societies. Mura and Sharif (2015) systematically analysed how researchers in six Southeast Asian countries (Malaysia, Singapore, Brunei, Indonesia, Thailand and Vietnam) 'do' and 'represent' tourism research. Their findings suggest that Southeast Asian researchers tend to favour quantitative methods over qualitative approaches. The authors duly described Asian tourism scholars as being 'religiously devoted to the most conventional rules dictated by positivist academic circles' (p. 12) developed in the West. Even when qualitative methods were used, the underpinning paradigms appear to be rather (post)positivistic. Using Denzin and Lincoln's (2011) terms, the authors conclude that the qualitative tourism research produced in Southeast Asia remains in the first three historical moments of qualitative research, which are known as the traditional period, the modernist phase, and the moment of blurred genres. Research produced in these periods has a strong emphasis on rigorous scientific approaches but lacks reflexivity, which is crucial when studying gender. Mura and Sharif's (2015) work forms an important basis of this chapter, which is also interested in the methodological aspect of tourism research in Asia. However, their work was limited to tourism scholars from six Southeast Asian countries, and they examined tourism research as a whole rather than focusing on any specific tourism sub-fields. We extend their study by focusing on tourism gender research in Asia.

Review of the Literature

Methods

This chapter examines the existing tourism research concerning Asian gender and Asian travel experience, focusing on authorship, research topic, and methodology. To ensure comparability, only articles published in tourism journals were considered. Book chapters, conference papers and other grey literature were excluded due to the limitations of existing databases and search engines. Because the language diversity in Asia is quite high, which rendering it impractical to extract and analyse articles in different languages, we considered only papers published in English-language journals. As mentioned in above, there is an increasing engagement of Asian tourism scholars in international scholarly discussion through English-language publications. We are interested in exploring what has been studied thus far by these scholars.

Unlike Mura and Sharif (2015), who extracted papers based on the list of tourism scholars in the selected countries, we referred to the list of tourism journals. So the first step was to identify a suitable 'list' or indices which have a comprehensive coverage of tourism journals. Past studies have considered different ranking systems and databases in identifying tourism papers for systematic literature reviews and bibliometric analyses. Some of the widely used indices and ranking systems include Scopus and ISI Web of Knowledge (e.g. Figueroa-Domecq et al., 2015) and SCImago Journal Rank (e.g. Hall, 2011). Other scholars reviewed papers from a list of journals without a clear justification of the selection criteria (e.g. Henderson & Gibson, 2013). For this chapter, we employed the Australian Business Deans Council (ABDC, 2013) Journal Quality List, which has been widely used in research for its wide coverage of tourism journals (Fennell, 2013; Hall, 2011); hence it is a credible reference.

In the ABDC list, 60 journals were coded as '1506', which is the research code for the field of tourism. After identifying the list of targeted journals, we did an initial review of the journals. During this stage, 12 journals were excluded because they are either non-tourism focused (e.g. event management and heritage journals), non-English-language or not listed in any scholarly databases, which precluded the next step, which was to run a systematic search using the search function of the database. The remaining 48 journals were examined using eight search terms – gender, female, male, women, men, masculinity, femininity and feminism. The first search was conducted in December 2014 and it was followed up in April 2015. Any article published after the cut-off date is not included in this chapter. Papers which contained any of the aforementioned terms in the title or among the identified keywords were selected; this resulted in 276 titles. We are interested in the first category of research listed by Figueroa-Domecq et al. (2015), which is 'gendered tourists'. Only papers which studied 'travel experience' were selected, resulting in 158 papers. Abstracts of the selected papers were read to identify studies which considered Asian travel experiences. This step significantly reduced the dataset, to only 24 papers. These papers were read closely and coded according to research topics and methodologies. Table 3.1 presents the list of authors, research topics and methodologies in that dataset.

Table 3.1 List of authors, research topics and methodologies

Year	Authors	Country	Research topic	Methodology
1994	Lang, Cheng-Te; O'Leary, Joseph T.; Morrison, Alastair M.	Japan	Activity segmentation of female travellers	Quantitative: secondary data analysis
1995	Creighton, Millie R.	Japan	Culture and gender identity	Qualitative: participant observation, interview
1999	Prakash, Indira J.	India	Senior women's perception of leisure	Qualitative: interview
2000	Cai, Liping A.; Combrink, Thomas E.	Japan	Female market segmentation	Quantitative: secondary data analysis
2000	Hashimoto, Atsuko	Japan	Female travel behaviour	Qualitative: archival research
2003	Cohen, Erik H.	Israel	Gender difference in destination image	Quantitative: survey
2006	Huang, Rong	China	Gender difference in travel behaviour	Mixed methods: survey, interview, focus group
2006	Poria, Yaniv	Israel and UK	Gay and lesbian hotel experience	Qualitative: interview
2006	Poria, Yaniv	Israel	Lesbian travel experience	Qualitative: narrative, diary analysis
2006	Teo, Peggy; Leong, Sandra	Asia	Gender performance in backpacking	Qualitative: site survey, interview, focus group, participant observation
2008	Noy, Chaim	Israel	Gender performance in backpacking	Qualitative: narrative, interview
2009	Okazaki, Shintaro; Hirose, Morikazu	Japan	Gender difference in travel information search	Quantitative: experiment
2010	Bokek-Cohen, Y.; Lissitsa, Sabina	Israe	Sexual manipulation in couples' vacation decision	Quantitative: survey
2011	Li, Mimi; Wen, Tong; Leung, Ariel	China	Female travel motivation	Quantitative: survey
2012	Kim, Myung-Ja; Lee, Myong Jae; Lee, Choong-Ki; Song, Hak-Jun	Korea	Gender effects in decision-making processes and overseas travel behaviour	Quantitative: online survey
2013	Asbollah, Asra Z.B.; Lade, Clare; Michael, Ewen	Malaysia	Muslim female tourist gaze	Qualitative: case study, participant observation

2013	Berdychevsky, Liza Poria, Yaniv Uriely, Natan	Israel	Female tourist sexual behaviour	Qualitative: constructivist grounded theory, interview
2013	Berdychevsky, Liza Gibson, Heather Poria, Yaniv	Israel	Female tourist sexual behaviour	Qualitative: constructivist grounded theory, interview
2013	Kim, Myung-Ja Lee, Choong-Ki Chung, Namho	Korea	Gender difference in online tourism shopping behaviour	Quantitative: online survey
2013	Wong, Ip K.A.	China	Gender difference in shopping preferences and service perceptions	Mixed methods: survey, interview
2014	Salim, Mona E. Osman Mohd T.	Iran	Gender difference in space usage	Quantitative: survey
2014	Zhang, Yang Hitchcock, Michael J.	China	Female tourist gaze	Qualitative, netnography, constructivist grounded theory, travel blog analysis
2015	Mustafa, Mairna H.	Jordan	Gender difference in travel behaviour	Quantitative: survey
2015	Tavakoli, Rokhshad Mura, Paolo	Iran	Women's behaviour a in virtual tourist destination	Qualitative: netnography, participant observation, interview

Findings and discussion

Authorship

Analysis of authorship focuses on the authors' gender and cultural background (Asian or non-Asian). This was ascertained by reviewing authors' profiles on university websites and professional social networks such as LinkedIn and ResearchGate. The findings suggest that Asian females formed the majority of lead authors, while one-third of the papers were led by Asian males. This can be interpreted as an encouraging outcome of the advances of Asian women's access to higher education and the rapid expansion of academic tourism schools and departments in Asia. Likewise, the ongoing feminist movements in some Asian countries may have nurtured feminist/gender interest in tourism research.

It appears that non-Asian authors generally contributed less than Asians based on the identified papers. For instance, there was not even one paper published by a non-Asian male as a single or lead author. While Asian scholars, who are the insiders, are more likely to provide in-depth understanding of the gendered travel behaviour of Asians by taking into account the underlying cultural differences, non-Asian scholars can provide outsider perspectives that may not be seen by insiders. Collaboration between the East and the West should be encouraged.

Nearly half of the selected papers (42%) were single authored. In terms of the number of papers written by single Asian authors, males and females made similar contributions. There was only one single-author paper written by non-Asian female but, as noted, none by non-Asian males. This finding resonates with Figueroa-Domecq et al. (2015), who also reported the phenomenon of lone gender researchers in tourism. Where Asian females were lead authors, diverse co-authorships were observed. They tended to have more collaboration with colleagues of the opposite sex, both Asians and non-Asians. However, Asian males had a tendency to work on their own or to select same-sex co-authors. The socio-cultural reasons why Asian males had not selected Asian females as their co-authors warrant further investigation. But based on our own experience, it is felt that the talent and capacity of Asian female scholars are often underrated until they prove themselves to be successful scholars with a good track record of publication. Hence, Asian male scholars are likely first to approach promising co-authors who are often male.

More than half (58%) of the selected papers were published in journals ranked in the top two quality classes – A* and A journals. The overall distribution was as follows: A*, 7; A, 7; B, 6; C, 4. *Annals of Tourism Research*, *Tourism Management*, *Asia Pacific Journal of Tourism Research* and *Tourism* are some of the main journals that had more publications on Asian gendered tourists. The majority of the papers with Asian females as lead authors were published in journals ranked A* ($n = 4$) and A ($n = 6$) and the one paper by a non-Asian female was in an A*-ranked journal. Asian males had three papers published in journals ranked in the top two quality classes (A*, 2; A, 1). While Mura and Sharif (2015) found that only a minority of articles produced by Asian tourism scholars made it into the top journals (i.e. A*- and A-ranked journals), our findings imply an opposite yet more optimistic scenario within the gender sub-field, as more than half of the papers identified in this study made it into the top two quality classes. All these papers were led by Asian authors (10 female, 3 male), with only one exception. This may seem oversimplified but gender research concerning Asian tourists may have the potential to be considered in high-quality journals because it addresses an under-researched area and provides important implications for the emerging Asian tourist markets.

Research topics

Figueroa-Domecq et al. (2015) classified tourism gender research into four categories: gendered tourists, gendered hosts, gendered labour, and theory, research and education. As mentioned, this chapter considers only studies relating to Asian travel experience, which falls into the first category – gendered tourists. Within this category, Figueroa-Domecq et al. (2015) found that consumer behaviour, decision-making and motivation have received more research attention than other topics. A similar trend was found in our analysis. Asian and non-Asian authors alike shared a similar interest in studying these areas. Specifically, travel behaviour appeared to be the most popular topic, including gender differences in travel behaviour and female tourist behaviour. The remaining papers covered a wide range of subjects, such as tourist gaze, travel motivation and travel information search, to name just a few. Analysis of the research topics against the background of the lead authors suggests that Asian male authors tended to focus on business aspects, such as market segmentation, shopping behaviour and destination image, while Asian female authors showed more interest in critical issues such as tourist sexual behaviour, gender performance and tourist gaze. Considering the social constructivist nature of gender, interestingly, the gender stereotypes have been reflected in the research topics as well. It appears that female researchers are more attracted to research that considers subjective emotions and embodied experiences, while male researchers are more inclined towards rational and positivistic research.

Female travel experience was the main research focus (58%) across the selected papers, followed by gender comparison studies. Research concerning Asian men's travel experience from a gendered perspective was almost undetectable. This finding lends support to prior research which has highlighted the dearth of tourism research on masculinities (Figueroa-Domecq et al., 2015; Thurnell-Read & Casey, 2014). The experience of male travellers appears to have been subsumed under gender comparison studies and gender-blind studies, with limited discussion on the construction and implication of masculinities. To a certain extent, due to the widespread recognition and criticism of the marginalisation of women's perspectives in research, the word 'gender' has been commonly used to refer to 'women only' (Ko et al., 2003). Likewise, the travel behaviour and experiences of LGBT (i.e. lesbian, gay, bisexual and transgender) consumers have received very limited attention in Asia, with few exceptions (see Poria, 2006a, 2006b). Study of this nature can be rather challenging and is discouraged in certain Asian countries for both religious and political reasons.

In addition to the lack of research on Asian men and LGBT tourists, our findings indicate two major gaps in research concerning gendered tourists in Asia. Firstly, we managed to locate only 24 journal articles in English, which is insufficient to understand the gendered travel experience of Asians. The identified papers considered tourists from eight Asian countries: China, India, Iran, Israel, Japan, Jordan, Korea and Malaysia. These countries account for less than a quarter (17%) of the 48 recognised countries in Asia (United Nations Statistics Division, 2013). Among these papers, there were seven studies on Israeli tourists and five studies on Japanese tourists.

This indicates that little is known about tourists from many other Asian countries. For example, tourism has begun to prosper in Dubai, Bahrain, Qatar and Saudi Arabia (Sherwood, 2006). Yet, limited research has been conducted to understand veiled Arab women and their behaviours, needs and preferences during holidays. Secondly, sex/romance tourism and tourist risk perception (e.g. tourist sexual harassment and violence) are important gender research topics (Figueroa-Domecq *et al.*, 2015) but have received little attention from Asian scholars. Although there were two papers on female tourist sexual behaviour, both were published by the same lead author, who is based in the United States, and they focused on a similar sample, namely of Israeli women. Perhaps due to the sensitive nature of these topics in a conservative social environment, Asian researchers may hesitate or be discouraged by their institutions to research these areas. Still, it is necessary to discuss the socio-cultural impact of these issues, particularly in Asia and specifically among Asians.

Methodology analysis

Table 3.2 summarises the methodologies and research approaches used in the selected papers. Contradicting previous reviews on gender research in tourism (Figueroa-Domecq *et al.*, 2015) and tourism research in Southeast Asia (Mura & Sharif, 2015), qualitative methods appear to be the dominant

Table 3.2 Methodologies

Methodology	No. of papers	% of papers
Qualitative	12	50%
Constructivist grounded theory	2	8%
Narrative	2	8%
Netnography	2	8%
General qualitative methods (interviews)	2	8%
Mixed of qualitative methods	2	8%
Case study	1	4%
Archival research	1	4%
Quantitative	10	42%
Survey	7	29%
Secondary data analysis	2	8%
Experiment	1	4%
Mixed methods	2	8%
Total	24	100%

methodology in investigating Asian gender and travel experience. Half ($n = 12$) of the selected articles were qualitative research which focused solely on women's travel experience, with only one exception – Poria (2006a) investigated the hotel experiences of gay and lesbian tourists. Many of these qualitative papers were exploratory in nature as the authors commonly revealed a dearth of research in their respective fields, for example virtual travel behaviour and women's sexual behaviour. Arguably, there are more studies employing qualitative methods because they were dealing with the travel experiences of under-researched groups such as Muslim women, Indian women, Israeli gay and lesbian tourists and Asian backpackers. Their voices have been silenced in the mainstream tourism research, mainly conducted by (white/male) researchers from the West using positivistic approaches. The interpretive nature of qualitative research gives voice to the previously silenced group, which is both Asian women and men, by presenting their accounts in their own voices.

As presented in Tables 3.1 and 3.2, a wide range of qualitative approaches were employed, some rather advanced. These include constructivist grounded theory, narrative (including diary analysis) and netnography. Although the authors appear to have embraced novel approaches in *doing* qualitative research, the *representations* appear to be fairly orthodox. For example, very few studies reported the researchers' personal and cultural backgrounds (Poria, 2006b; Tavakoli & Mura, 2015) and only one study was written in the first person (Noy, 2008). The majority of these qualitative papers did not present the authors' ontological and epistemological stance. Judging from the representation styles, evaluation criteria and discussion of subjectivity (or bias), many of these studies are located in the first three periods of qualitative research (Denzin & Lincoln, 2011).

Across the 24 articles, 10 employed quantitative methods, including questionnaire survey, secondary data analysis and experiment. Gender comparison and the effect of gender were the main research foci for these quantitative papers. The common analysis techniques used included factor analysis, structural equation modelling, *t*-test, cluster analysis and descriptive statistics. Exceptions of quantitative papers which focused solely on Asian women's experiences include those by Lang *et al.* (1994), who used activity segmentation to identify five groups of Japanese female tourists, and Li *et al.* (2011), who studied the travel motivations of Chinese women in terms of push–pull motivational factors. None of the quantitative papers addressed their ontological and epistemological stance, and by default assumed a positivist or post-positivist paradigm.

A number of observations were made from the analysis of methodologies. First of all, we envisage that qualitative approaches will continue to be favoured until tourism scholars have gained substantial knowledge concerning Asian gender. Second, there is a huge potential for gender researchers in Asia to challenge orthodox tourism research, which is dominated by the positivist perspective (Figueroa-Domecq et al., 2015) and, hence, has limited capacity in understanding the underlying meanings and complications of tourist behaviour (Morgan & Pritchard, 2005). The existing gendered tourism research appears to have been trapped within the first three moments of qualitative research. One way to break through this glass ceiling is to embrace critical and reflexive approaches which have been widely embraced by feminist researchers in other social science disciplines. Another way is to look into our own cultural and knowledge systems to learn about alternative and localised ways of knowing and knowledge production rather than embracing Western ideologies indiscriminately without questioning whether they are applicable to Asian contexts. Applying a postcolonial or even a decolonised lens (Chambers & Buzinde, 2015) when investigating Asian genders in tourism might be a solution. To begin with, Asian tourism researchers are encouraged to reflect on and discuss explicitly their ontological and epistemological stance, which is currently lacking.

Reflection and Conclusion

The study has thus far answered the questions we put forth earlier. We have learnt that only a handful of papers concerning Asian, gender and tourist experience have been published in internationally recognised tourism journals. Within this set of papers, we found an encouraging phenomenon: Asian female researchers were the major lead authors. We have identified topics that have been studied thus far and gender differences in choosing research topics. This study has also identified gaps which can be explored in future studies, especially those concerning Asian men and masculinities, and LGBT tourists from Asia. Methodologically, it is found that qualitative methods remain the dominant in studying this under-researched area, but we also observed a lack of reflexivity in these qualitative papers and many authors were still avoiding writing themselves into the paper. Here we challenge the conventional way of representing research by revealing our experience as novice Asian female researchers in this short reflexive conclusion. Our reflection focuses on freedom in research, and language, which are the two main limitations influencing Asian gender researchers in tourism.

Freedom in research

While researchers are free to conduct any kind of research as long as ethical procedures are adhered to (although some Asian institutions may not even have a research ethic committee), the choice of topics often involves consideration of funding and opportunity for publication. We both have experiences of giving up researching gender issues because of the need to secure research funding. When researching in Malaysia, Elaine had always wanted to study the gendered risk perceptions of Asian female travellers, but was advised against doing so, as gender research was thought to limit her future career opportunity in Malaysian tourism academia and she subsequently changed her topic in order to receive research funding. It is only when she moved to Australia that she reinstated her research interest in Asian female travellers. Rokhshad has realised in retrospect that she has considered a number of issues regarding the selection of sensitive topics. At first, she wondered why there is an unbelievable gap in gender-related studies and thought someone should start writing about these matters. As she began research on Iranian female travellers, she found herself turning away from sensitive issues such as veiling and homosexuality to avoid the social consequences of her research outcomes. Some scholars in her home country, Iran, may have also wanted to research these topics, but could have been stopped by university committees and been advised to change their topics. As Rokhshad was studying in Malaysia at that time, she had more freedom because of the social environment. However, she was still concerned about publishing the findings. Although both of us have not researched LGBT tourists, homosexuality is illegal in both Malaysia and Iran. Publication of this nature is highly sensitive as it may involve criticism of political and religious stances, which may have social and/or legal consequences which will affect one's career. Hence, freedom of research is limited in some Asian countries and this may encourage researchers to be more conservative in choosing a research topic.

In addition to topic choice, how we should 'do' and 'represent' the research is another complex issue to grapple with. Based on our experiences in Asia, too often we see positivistic quantitative research being cherished and interpretive qualitative research being criticised. When Elaine was interviewed for a PhD scholarship, her examiner insisted on her spelling out the *variables*, despite her explaining that the *constructs* would emerge later from the data. Likewise, Rokhshad was asked to validate her qualitative data and to prove the reliability of her findings. When it comes to publication, we are often reminded by our advisers and colleagues, and sometimes by reviewers, that showing personal stance and emotion by writing in the first person is biased and destructive to the credibility of the research. The understanding that there is no value-free research has been debated in Western academia (Neuman, 2011; Wright, 2010). We hope to see more Asian tourism gender scholars engaging in this conversation and to start challenging the conventions by critically reflecting on their own research practices and the underlying philosophical assumptions.

Language

The language barrier is an important factor that has impeded Asian scholars from engaging in international tourism discourse. Asian scholars may have submitted papers to high-ranking journals but received desk rejection because of their inadequate command of the English language. This has happened to us and many of our fellow Asian colleagues. Park *et al.* (2011) analysed articles published in the six most cited hospitality and tourism journals between 2000 and 2009 and found that over 50% of the papers emerged from three English-speaking nations, namely the United States, the United Kingdom and Australia. This is essentially a representation of the colonisation of knowledge dissemination, as only papers published in high-impact journals, which are predominantly in English, are considered high-quality research. But to be accepted in those journals, a paper has to be written in good English, even if English is the author's second or third language. Novice researchers like us are often advised to use an editing and proofreading service, but this is expensive, especially for scholars from developing Asian countries, where services of this nature are not commonly provided or subsidised by universities. Accordingly, we invite readers to reflect on whether the existing publishing practices are fair to Asian scholars. It is beyond the scope of this chapter to find a solution to these perpetuated norms, but a possible way out is to recognise the quality of the research rather than the quality of the writing. After all, we are talking about tourism journals, not English literary journals. Perhaps more outlets for a shorter summary piece (e.g. research notes) that highlights the main findings and key arguments can help overcome the language obstacle. However, this can be achieved only with institutional provision, as research notes are currently not taken into account in the performance appraisals of academic staff members in many universities. At the same time, more recognition is needed for journals and papers written in languages other than English. Journal editors and publishers may consider providing complimentary translation and/or proofreading services to non-English-speaking authors.

Limitations of the study

We are aware of the existence of research papers on Asian tourists and gender published in non-English journals, but it is impossible to extract them due to the diversity of languages used in Asia. So we limited our selection to English-language tourism journals in the ABDC list to enable a 'systematic' identification of papers. This, however, represents the main limitation of the current review. Besides, tourism is a multidisciplinary field and, thus, many papers related to gendered tourists have been published in non-tourism journals (see Holliday *et al.*, 2015; Ormond, 2015). These papers are not captured in this chapter. Moreover, we used gender-based phrases (i.e. gender, female, male, women, men, masculinity, femininity, and feminism), as suggested by Henderson and Gibson (2013), to filter the articles. Papers which are relevant to our research interest but did not contain any of these search terms in their titles nor in their keywords may have been overlooked. Despite these limitations, this review has depicted the landscape of gendered tourist studies in Asia, and provided suggestions for future research. We hope this chapter can enthuse more researchers to explore this exciting sub-field – tourism gender research in Asia.

References

ABDC (2013) ABDC journal quality list 2013. At http://www.abdc.edu.au/pages/abdc-journal-quality-list-2013.html (accessed May 2016).

Asbollah, A.Z.B., Lade, C. and Michael, E. (2013) The tourist's gaze: From the perspective of a Muslim woman. *Tourism Analysis* 18 (6), 677–690. doi: 10.3727/108354213X13824558188703.

Berdychevsky, L., Gibson, H. and Poria, Y. (2013) Women's sexual behavior in tourism: Loosening the bridle. *Annals of Tourism Research* 42, 65–85. doi: 10.1016/j.annals.2013.01.006.

Berdychevsky, L., Poria, Y. and Uriely, N. (2013) Sexual behavior in women's tourist experiences: Motivations, behaviors, and meanings. *Tourism Management* 35, 144–155. doi: 10.1016/j.tourman.2012.06.011.

Bokek-Cohen, Y. and Lissitsa, S. (2010) Sex: The power of the powerless? The use of sex as a spousal influence strategy in vacation purchase decisions. *Asia Pacific Journal of Tourism Research* 15 (4), 431–448. doi: 10.1080/10941665.2010.520946.

Cai, L.A. and Combrink, T.E. (2000) Japanese female travelers: A unique outbound market. *Asia Pacific Journal of Tourism Research* 5 (1), 16–24. doi: 10.1080/10941660008722055.

Chambers, D. and Buzinde, C. (2015) Tourism and decolonisation: Locating research and self. *Annals of Tourism Research* 51, 1–16. doi: 10.1016/j.annals.2014.12.002.

Cohen, E.H. (2003) Images of Israel: A structural comparison along gender, ethnic, denominational and national lines. *Tourist Studies* 3 (3), 253–280. doi: 10.1177/1468797603049659.

Creighton, M.R. (1995) Japanese craft tourism: Liberating the crane wife. *Annals of Tourism Research* 22 (2), 463–478. doi: 10.1016/0160-7383(94)00086-7.

Denzin, N.K. and Lincoln, Y.S. (eds) (2011) *The SAGE Handbook of Qualitative Research* (4th editon). Thousand Oaks, CA: Sage.

Fennell, D. (2013) The ethics of excellence in tourism research. *Journal of Travel Research* 52 (4), 417–425. doi: 10.1177/0047287512475220.

Figueroa-Domecq, C., Pritchard, A., Segovia-Pérez, M., Morgan, N. and Villacé-Molinero, T. (2015) Tourism gender research: A critical accounting. *Annals of Tourism Research* 52, 87–103. doi: 10.1016/j.annals.2015.02.001.

Hall, M.C. (2011) Publish and perish? Bibliometric analysis, journal ranking and the assessment of research quality in tourism. *Tourism Management* 32 (1), 16–27. doi: 10.1016/j.tourman.2010.07.001.

Hashimoto, A. (2000) Young Japanese female tourists: An in-depth understanding of a market segment. *Current Issues in Tourism* 3 (1), 35–50. doi: 10.1080/13683500000866/865.

Henderson, K.A. and Gibson, H.J. (2013) An integrative review of women, gender, and leisure: Increasing complexities. *Journal of Leisure Research* 45 (2), 115–135.

Henderson, K.A. and Hickerson, B. (2007) Women and leisure: Premises and performances uncovered in an integrative review. *Journal of Leisure Research* 39 (4), 591–610.

Holliday, R., Bell, D., Cheung, O., Jones, M. and Probyn, E. (2015) Brief encounters: Assembling cosmetic surgery tourism. *Social Science and Medicine* 124 (0), 298–304. doi: 10.1016/j.socscimed.2014.06.047.

Hsu, C.H.C. (2015) Tourism and hospitality education in Asia. In D. Dredge, D. Airey and M. J. Gross (eds) *The Routledge Handbook of Tourism and Hospitality Education* (pp. 197–209). New York: Routledge.

Huang, R. (2006) A study of gender differences: The travel behaviour of Chinese international students studying in the UK. *Tourism* 54 (1), 63–69.

Kim, M.-J., Lee, C.-K. and Chung, N. (2013) Investigating the role of trust and gender in online tourism shopping in South Korea. *Journal of Hospitality and Tourism Research* 37 (3), 377–401. doi: 10.1177/1096348012436377.

Kim, M.-J., Lee, M.J., Lee, C.-K. and Song, H.-J. (2012) Does gender affect Korean tourists' overseas travel? Applying the model of goal-directed behavior. *Asia Pacific Journal of Tourism Research* 17 (5), 509–533. doi: 10.1080/10941665.2011.627355.

Ko, D., Haboush, J.K. and Piggott, J.R. (eds) (2003) *Women and Confucian Cultures in Premodern China, Korea, and Japan*. Los Angeles, CA: University of California Press.

Lang, C.-T., O'Leary, J.T. and Morrison, A.M. (1994) Activity segmentation of Japanese female overseas travelers. *Journal of Travel and Tourism Marketing* 2 (4), 1–22. doi: 10.1300/J073v02n04_01.

Li, M., Wen, T. and Leung, A. (2011) An exploratory study of the travel motivation of Chinese female outbound tourists. *Journal of China Tourism Research* 7 (4), 411–424. doi: 10.1080/19388160. 2011.627020.

Mok, K.H. (2007) Questing for internationalization of universities in Asia: Critical reflections. *Journal of Studies in International Education* 11 (3–4), 433–454. doi: 10.1177/1028315306291945.

Morgan, N. and Pritchard, A. (2005) On souvenirs and metonymy: Narratives of memory, metaphor and materiality. *Tourist Studies* 5 (1), 29–53. doi: 10.1177/1468797605062714.

Mura, P. and Sharif, S.P. (2015) The crisis of the 'crisis of representation' – Mapping qualitative tourism research in Southeast Asia. *Current Issues in Tourism*, 1–17. doi: 10.1080/13683500.2015. 1045459.

Mustafa, M.H. (2015) Gender and behavior in archaeological sites. *International Journal of Hospitality and Tourism Administration* 16 (2), 183–201. doi: 10.1080/15256480.2015.1023665.

Neuman, W.L. (2011) *Social Research Methods: Qualitative and Quantitative Approaches*. Boston, MA: Pearson Education.

Noy, C. (2008) Traversing hegemony: Gender, body, and identity in the narratives of Israeli female backpackers. *Tourism Review International* 12 (2), 93–114.

Okazaki, S. and Hirose, M. (2009) Does gender affect media choice in travel information search? On the use of mobile Internet. *Tourism Management* 30 (6), 794–804. doi: 10.1016/j.tourman.2008.12.012.

Ormond, M. (2015) En route: Transport and embodiment in international medical travel journeys between Indonesia and Malaysia. *Mobilities* 10 (2), 285–303. doi: 10.1080/17450101.2013.857812.

Park, K., Phillips, W.J., Canter, D.D. and Abbott, J. (2011) Hospitality and tourism research rankings by author, university, and country using six major journals: The first decade of the new millennium. *Journal of Hospitality and Tourism Research* 35 (3), 381–416. doi: 10.1177/1096348011400743.

Poria, Y. (2006a) Assessing gay men and lesbian women's hotel experiences: An exploratory study of sexual orientation in the travel industry. *Journal of Travel Research* 44 (3), 327–334. doi: 10.1177 /0047287505279110.

Poria, Y. (2006b) Tourism and spaces of anonymity: An Israeli lesbian woman's travel experience. *Tourism* 54 (1), 33–42.

Prakash, I.J. (1999) Senior women's perception of leisure in India. *Tourism Recreation Research* 24 (1), 82–85. doi: 10.1080/02508281.1999.11014862.

Pritchard, A., Morgan, N., Ateljevic, I. and Harris, C. (2007) Editors' introduction: Tourism, gender, embodiment and experience. In A. Pritchard, N. Morgan, I. Ateljevic and C. Harris (eds) *Tourism and Gender: Embodiment, Sensuality, and Experience* (pp. 1–12). Wallingford: CABI.

Salim, M.E. and Tahir, O.M. (2014) Gender affecting tourists' needs for a public open space Case study: Kish Island, Iran. *Tourism* 62, 63–73.

Sherwood, S. (2006) Is Qatar the next Dubai? *New York Times*, 4 June. Available at http://www.nytimes.com/2006/06/04/travel/04qatar.html?_r=1&pagewanted=all& (accessed May 2016).

Smith, V.L. (1979) Women the taste-makers in tourism. *Annals of Tourism Research* 6 (1), 49–60. doi: 10.1016/0160-7383(79)90094-X.

Swain, M.B. (1995) Gender in tourism. *Annals of Tourism Research* 22 (2), 247–266. doi: 10.1016/0160-7383(94)00095-6.

Tavakoli, R. and Mura, P. (2015) 'Journeys in Second Life' – Iranian Muslim women's behaviour in virtual tourist destinations. *Tourism Management* 46, 398–407. doi: 10.1016/j.tourman.2014.07.015.

Teo, P. and Leong, S. (2006) A postcolonial analysis of backpacking. *Annals of Tourism Research* 33 (1), 109–131. doi: 10.1016/j.annals.2005.05.001.

Thurnell-Read, T. and Casey, M. (eds) (2014) *Men, Masculinities, Travel and Tourism*. Basingstoke: Palgrave Macmillan.

Tribe, J. (2010) Tribes, territories and networks in the tourism academy. *Annals of Tourism Research* 37 (1), 7–33. doi: 10.1016/j.annals.2009.05.001.

United Nations Statistics Division (2013) Composition of macro geographical (continental) regions, geographical sub-regions, and selected economic and other groupings. At http://unstats.un.org/unsd/methods/m49/m49regin.htm (accessed May 2016).

Wilson, E. (2004) A 'journey of her own'? The impact of constraints on women's solo travel. Doctoral dissertation. Available at https://www120.secure.griffith.edu.au/rch/items/4b2568ae-351605f7bbc73acd 31f17b1c/1 (accessed May 2016).

Wong, I.K.A. (2013) Mainland Chinese shopping preferences and service perceptions in the Asian gaming destination of Macau. *Journal of Vacation Marketing* 19 (3), 239–251. doi: 10.1177/1356766712459737.

Wright, R.K. (2010) 'Been there, done that': Embracing our post-trip experiential recollections through the social construction and subjective consumption of personal narratives. In M. Morgan, P. Lugosi and J.R.B. Ritchie (eds) *The Tourism and Leisure Experience* (pp. 99–116). Bristol: Channel View Publications.

Zhang, Y. and Hitchcock, M.J. (2014) The Chinese female tourist gaze: A netnography of young women's blogs on Macao. *Current Issues in Tourism*, advance online publication doi: 10.1080/13683500.2014.904845.

4 Asian Gendered Performance in Tourism

Tau Sian Lim and Paolo Mura

> *Gender is an act which has been rehearsed, much as a script survives the particular actors who make use of it, but which requires individual actors in order to be actualised and reproduced as reality once again.*
> (Butler, 1988: 526).

> *We understand social life as narrative, image, crisis and crisis resolution, drama, person-to-person interaction, display behaviour, and so on.*
> (Schechner, 1985: 62)

Introduction

As Richard Schechner puts it, our lives are performances in which social agents enact roles. Considering our ability to perform multiple roles simultaneously, an enacted role will then be active at a specific moment in time and contextualised in a particular setting. Performances evoke ideas of *bodies performing*, bodies talking, moving, acting, expressing emotions. As such, the *corporeality* of performances cannot transcend the existence of physical bodies enacting performances. Nonetheless, the basis of *physicality* and *corporeality* should not warrant essentialists to conclude that *bodies* are merely biologically determined. Departing from Michel Foucault's (1977) idea that bodies are *historically produced* and Cliffort Geertz's (1973) work on the relationship between bodies and culture, Errington (1990) points out that 'human bodies and the cultures in which they grow cannot be separated conceptually without seriously misconstruing the nature of each' (p. 14). In other words, forms of embodiment are far from being a sole product of genetic makeups. Rather, they are socially, culturally, politically and contextually constructed and reproduced. Importantly, the social construction and representation of the body are gendered laden and produce *male* and *female* forms of embodiment and gendered performances. This process occurs in any social and cultural context, including in Asian societies.

Asia covers a vast geographical area and there are immense differences in the degree to which different regions have been modernised. The inferences of the notion 'Asian' are often used in combination with cultures, traditions and religious practices, which evidently make the intra-Asian differences greater. Therefore, when the notion 'Asian' is used in conjunction with a wider cultural, historical and geographical category, its designation becomes rather empty. Consequently, to reduce the notion of 'Asian' to an individual from any of the Asian geographical regions seems simplistic. The connotation becomes more problematic when used in parallel with gender. But beyond vague geographical generalisations, is there any recognisable Asian gendered performance in tourism settings? This chapter aims to answer this question. The performance of a tourist on a beach holiday as a social agent is reflexively narrated through the eyes of an Asian scholar in order to explore the embodiment and enactment of gendered performances.

I am a Malaysian Chinese male lecturer and PhD scholar based at a Malaysian university. While my voice dominates the narrative as a first-person speaker to represent and reflect upon my own tourist experiences, I need to acknowledge that this chapter is the result of an intellectual venture I embarked on together with Paolo, my mentor and colleague. Paolo is an Italian lecturer who, after completing his doctoral studies in New Zealand, moved to Malaysia. In the last six years, he has been holding a lecturer position in tourism at a Malaysian private university. At the current time, he is also conducting research on Asian gendered identities in tourism.

In July 2015, Paolo approached me and asked if I would collaborate with him in writing a chapter on Asian gendered performances in tourism settings. He had then written a partial draft centred on the main theoretical approaches about gender, performance and performativity. However, he faced setbacks in relating all this body of knowledge to tourism, particularly within the context of Asian holiday experiences. As an Italian, his six-year residency in Malaysia, a Southeast Asian country that prides itself on being 'truly Asia', had granted him a good understanding of 'Asia' and 'Asianness'. Yet, he is not 'Asian' and my being a co-author would be the best collaborative solution. Perhaps it was the initial excitement that blinded us to a recognition of the complexity of 'Asian' my being born Asian may have given us the false sense that I had understood something about being Asian, when, in fact, being one all my life, I had yet to fully comprehend its meanings. During our occasional lunch meetings, Paolo and I discussed and debated a few key questions. Was 'Asian' supposed to be a sharp contrast to 'Western', whereby the 'Asianness' in being non-Western would suggest I should be knowledgeable about being Asian? If by 'Asian' we mean individuals from Asia, then would my Asian origin unconditionally substantiate this claim? These questions regularly challenged our theoretical beliefs, paradigmatic assumptions and perceptions of our 'selves'. Paolo then asked me to describe and reflect upon my holiday experiences based on Richard Schechner's studies on anthropology and theatre, Judith Butler's (1988) work on gender and performativity, as well as Victor Turner's (1969) writings on the ritual process. This invitation marked the beginning of a collaborative journey and this chapter represents the final stage of this intellectual venture. But we both agreed that reflecting upon our own tourism experiences would be a never-ending journey; it would also be a never-ending quest for knowledge.

This chapter is reflexive and embodied in nature, an approach that took effect after the critical turn in tourism studies (Ateljevic *et al.*, 2005), producing what Tribe (2005) claims to be the *new* tourism research. This critical turn, through the paradigm of post-structuralism, enables marginalised representations of *self* in writing to move progressively to mainstream qualitative research (Denzin & Lincoln, 2011) and embraces research topics such as gender and body (Abramovici, 2007). Reflexivity in this chapter is based on the idea of embodiment, which challenges the perceived neutrality of disembodied constructions of knowledge in the tourism and leisure fields (Abramovici, 2007; Aitchison, 2001; Johnston, 2001; Veijola & Jokinen, 1994). Along with this idea and the emerging new metaphors in tourism enquiry, the reflexivity approach in this chapter aims to conceptualise the notion of *gendered performance* in the context of tourism and I am reflexively writing by engaging here with three frameworks: *embodiment*, *performativity* and *performance*. The embodiment framework, as explained by Ateljevic *et al.* (2005) and Grosz (1994), is used to address the issues of me and the embodiment of gender as a social construction, while the reference to Butler's (1988) performativity framework is to contend that our gender is constructed through our own repetitive performance of gender. The performance framework originating from Goffman (1959) is used to explore and explain how, through performance in front of a specific audience, the actor gives meaning to himself, to others and to the situation. In tourism research, Goffman's performance framework has been used to examine different *visiting* performances on the Taj Mahal stage (Edensor, 1998), *backpacking* performance on the resort stage in Fiji (Doome & Ateljevic, 2005) and *tanning* performance on the beach stage in Italy (Abramovici, 2007).

While the idea that Asian genders and performances are interwoven has been contemplated by both Asian and non-Asian scholars (Hatley, 1990; Rodgers, 1990; Tsing, 1990), little has been written on Asian gendered performances by tourism scholars. For this reason, this chapter details an Asian scholar's reflexive narration as an approach to understanding the Asian gendered performance by exploring the symbolism of Asian femininity and skin colour, particularly *tanning* performance. In this context, I reflexively narrate the beach as a *stage* for the tanning performance, to link the symbolic meanings of complexion and femininity in Asia with gender and performance. The reason to contextualise tanning performance is a personal one, related to my personal experience with gender trouble due to skin colour. As tanning is almost by definition a part of any beach vacation but is also generally a contradiction to the symbolic femininity of being fair skinned, it is by exploring this paradox that this chapter aims to discover how it affects the performance of gender in tourism.

It is not my intention to generalise or to claim my complete understanding of Asian 'genders'. The Asian gendered performance that I experienced appeared to indicate a set of certain characteristics, which were often repeatedly manifested, especially within a particular tourism setting. My journey into the understanding of that Asian gendered performance involved reflecting upon my learned experience and observations of the people who crossed path with my own history, culture and tradition. It was by narrating those reflections on ideas of gender and performance that I gained a personal understanding of one of the performances that defined Asian gender in tourism, while at the same time such self-reflections open up the possibility of observing the Asian gendered performance through my eyes. In view of the personal nature of my narrative, my positionality and embodiment as the narrator of this reflexive writing are acknowledged as the key aspect of my methodology. It is impossible to divorce myself from the background that influences my value-laden analysis and privileges me with my social position of authoring (Ateljevic *et al.*, 2005). The body as the inscriptive surface reflects my positionality as the choreography of knowledge based on my gender, sex, class, race and nationality (Grosz, 1994).

I continue this chapter with my embodiment, a reflection and theoretical presentation of the way gender is linked to performance. I then move to a discussion of how gendered selves are related to corporeal acts, and introduce the concept of performativity. I explain my embodiment and prescribed gendered lenses by presenting the association between skin colour and femininity within my Asian communities. Studying tanning in the context of femininity, it is necessary to make known how I came to understand the way skin colour influences gendered performance within the socially constructed reality of gender. This chapter draws on the metaphor of theatrical performance as a framework to explore tanning as a form of gendered performance. The key focus here is on the performance staged at the front of what commonly comprises setting, appearance and manner, which form the backdrop for a performer to play a part and present a character to an audience with dramatic realisation in order to achieve idealisation in tanning performance.

My Embodiment: Gendered Performances and Performative Acts

When I was a child growing up in Malaysia, my mum was always very careful about preventing me and my three brothers from spending a lot of time in the sun. It was easier for her to rationalise this by saying that we would fall sick as a consequence, rather than expressing her concerns about how our neighbours would associate our dark complexion with peasants from a poor village. As an Indonesian with a dark complexion herself, my mum learned through socialisation that skin colour played an indicator of class within our neighbourhood, particularly within the Malaysian Chinese community. Despite being an Indonesian Chinese, her Chinese heritage had never been truly recognised by our neighbours, as her relatively dark complexion purportedly marked her as a labourer, a stereotypical Indonesian maid who was generally found working in Malaysia. I was too young to find that sentiment offensive but had long been internalising that skin colour functioned as an indicator of socio-economic status. I was lighter-skinned than my brothers and so had gained favouritism as a child from relatives and elders who prized lightness. However, this preference appeared to wane when I reached my teenage years, the years when my masculinity and femininity turned into binary concepts, when masculinity was correlated with tanned skin femininity with lighter skin. Consequently, the socio-economic status designated by skin colour became secondary when normative expectation of congruence between tanned skin and masculinity began to dominate my everyday life.

Understanding the relationship between gender and performance requires a discussion of the role of the body in performing (production and expression) gendered identities and practices. Butler (1988) points out that gendered performances should not be conceived as *monolithic* representations. Rather, individuals learn how to act the 'proper' gendered performance based on the context and historical time. An individual learns how to perform his or her expected gender properly through societal punishments and rewards. Masculine identities, for example, are produced and learnt through specific performances in non-theatrical settings. When gendered selves are not properly performed (e.g. according to the specific socio-cultural context), gendered enactments may be labelled as deviant, as they do not conform to what Butler (1988) refers to as 'the illusion of gender essentialism' (p. 528).

As a teenager, I was made aware of the 'appropriate' masculine performances to be enacted in both private and public spheres and was discouraged to perform what are socially constructed as 'unmasculine' acts. For example, shying away from the sun was seen as feminine, and my doing so during my teenage years had therefore labelled me as feminine. My reluctance to actively participate in sports and tan, that is, to perform masculinity in socially and culturally determined masculine ways, was perceived as disruptive to social and cultural norms.

By contending that gendered selves are not ontologically disentangled from their performances, Butler (1988) breaks the causal nexus between identity and its performance. As she explains, 'because gender is not a fact, the various acts of gender creates the idea of gender, and without those acts, there would be no gender at all' (p. 522). Furthermore, she contends that, '[g]ender is in no way a stable identity or locus of agency from which various acts proceed; rather, it is an identity tenuously constituted in time – an identity instituted through a *stylised repetition of act*' (p. 519; original emphasis). As such, acts of gender are *performative* as they *produce*, *define* and *represent* gendered identities. Importantly, it needs to be recognised that the formation of gendered identities through performative acts is politically, historically, culturally and socially determined (Butler, 1988).

When I reflected on Butler's theory and my own experiences, tanning as a performative act of hegemonic masculinity was embodied in the ideal of being masculine, one that was founded on gender discourses of active participation in sports during my teenage years. These 'masculine' activities, which in most cases tanned the body as they required long hours in the hot sun, were bodily practices pursued fervently by alpha males in my institutions. Therefore, the dominant masculine quality of these embodied and engendered activities had politically, historically, culturally and socially helped to construct and legitimise tanning as a type of masculine performative act in my life.

My embodiment, gender identity and gendered performances have enabled me to position myself within the tourism enquiry and to reflexively narrate the relation between skin colour and performative acts, which provide the background for the Asian gendered performance in this chapter. These explanations are crucial to better contextualise and understand tanning through my socio-cultural lense, for they form the backdrop and set the scene for the beach, the stage on which the tanning performance takes place. The whole performance of tanning can now be seen in the context of (my) Asian society, as narrated in the next section of this chapter. The narrative is explored and analysed using Goffman's (1959) framework, which is rooted in the metaphor of theatrical performance.

Gendered Performances: Sun Tanning and Screening at the Beach

Goffman (1959) uses the term 'performances' to refer to 'all the activity of a given participant on a given occasion which serves to influence in any way any of the other participants' (p. 15). He states that the front-stage, or simply the *front*, is central in a performance, as it is the region on stage where an individual performs the prescribed routine to define the situation for the audience. He describes the standard parts of the front, consisting primarily of a *setting*, which comprises 'furniture, décor, physical layout, and other background items which supply the scenery and stage props for the spate of human action played out before, within, or upon it' (p. 22). A *setting* tends to be geographically rooted within a confined space, so that those who perform are unable to begin their performance until they have gone to the specified location and must end their performance when they leave it. In the context of the beach, I reflexively narrate the scenery and stage props as a *setting* for tanning performance.

The weather was blisteringly hot and my backpack suddenly felt a ton heavier. I struggled to keep it steady while fighting to wipe away the sweat trailing down my back. In the blazing heat of the relentless sun, I was drenched in sweat. I felt enormously relieved when we finally halted to take refuge in the shelter of a hut. As I took a deep breath, a familiar scent filled my nostrils. I was greeted by the unmistakeable salty smell of the sea. Shaped like a cotton ball, the clouds came over the sun momentarily and a gentle breeze blew. It touched the cheek of my face and I felt a sense of tranquillity. As I began to relax and cool down. I started to soak in the view of the surrounding area. The surroundings, crowded with tourists, created a certain vibe and energy on this pristine beach. Tilting like the earth on its axis, the towering palm trees fringed the shoreline and made an array of indelible landmarks. Despite the scorching sun, young children and parents embraced its warmth and were seen playing in the water and on the beach. The silky rich sand fell noticeably into their footprints while they were taking a barefoot stroll. The surrounding was filled with laughter accompanied by the sound of the waves lapping against the sand. I tried to stare out across the glittering sea but the blinding sun looked down unforgivingly and continuously glaring on it, causing my eyes to squint while, at the same time, like a scorching oven, baking the tourists who were sunbathing on the sweltering beach. Simultaneously, its rays danced amid the leaves of the tilting palm trees, creating shadows of cool bliss for tourists seeking sanctuary from the heat.

Apart from the *setting*, the front also consists of a *personal front*, a set of characteristics that reflects the identity of the performer, which may include 'clothing; sex, age, and racial characteristics; size and looks; posture; speech patterns; facial expressions; bodily gestures; and the like' (Goffman, 1959: 24). Personal front can be aptly divided into *appearance* and *manner*. The former refers to the performer's social status or temporary ritual state, that is, whether she or he is engaging in formal or social activities, while the latter refers to the interaction role the performer is assumed to play in the oncoming scene.

> *At the beach, it was a common sight to see half-naked men in shorts or Caucasian women scantily clad in bikinis. They were the sunbathers who worshipped the sun and enjoyed every opportunity to get a tan. In order to ensure no visibility of white marks on their backs, some of the women even laid on their fronts with bikini tops unclasped, a sight that caused some raised eyebrows from those who disapproved of such a provocative act while instantaneously welcomed unabashed staring from ardent onlookers who feasted their eyes on it. Tanning being a personal activity could be seen as performed in a temporarily ritual state of stillness, with almost absolute muteness. Contrasting with these scantily clad women were the fully clothed Asian tourists sitting on the sand, with hats covering their faces. They took shelter under shady trees and sought every opportunity to shield their faces and body parts from the assault of the blazing sun. Sunscreen lotion was applied liberally, preventing their porcelain skin from darkening. While the exposed body was creamed up with gentle, massaging motions, they were seen to engage in casual conversations with their companions.*

Taking a given participant and her performance as a basis of reference, Goffman (1959) refers to those who contribute to the other performances as the *audience*, *observers* or *co-participants*, while the prearranged stylised action which takes place during a performance and possibly on other occasions is referred to as a *part* or *routine*. He further states that, at any given time, individuals and groups are both the performers and the audience, performing and observing on specific stages where they are playing different parts on the back-stage and front-stage. In line with this, I will explore my narrative of tanning performance by identifying how the part a tourist performs on the beach 'stage' is tailored to the parts performed by the others present, and yet these others also constitute the audience.

> *The stage was the beach and I, as one of the actors, walked onto the scene. I took refuge in the shelter of a hut, preparing to become one of the front-stage performers of tanning. I observed the beach to take in who the other performers were, how their bodies were arranged on the beach and where they positioned themselves. I took in the men's and women's appearances on the beach, the half-naked men in shorts and the scantily clad women in bikinis. I looked at*

other performers who were looking at each other on the beach. I also looked at the contrast of other performers, who were (not) performing tanning by applying sunscreen lotion under the shady trees. Without my realisation, some other performers were looking at me, diverting their attention from those who were already on the beach scene. They were the performers whom I was the audience for when I walked onto the beach stage. The roles had reversed. My new character when I walked onto the beach stage had sent visual signals to my audience through my costume and props: the way I was dressed, the way I looked, and the way I walked towards my chosen spot.

During a performance, an individual will usually present signs which dramatically highlight and display confirmatory facts that might otherwise remain ambiguous. This dramatisation is important because when individuals play a part they implicitly require their audience to be impressed by the performance. The audience is asked to believe that the character they observe essentially owns the qualities that character appears to own, that the part she or he performs will have the effects that are implicitly called for, and that, as a whole, matters are what they seem to be. Therefore, a performer is known to offer a performance and to put on a show for the benefits of others (Goffman, 1959).

Having introduced the importance of dramatic realisation in performance, I will now describe tanning performance, which entails a set of performative acts that may be regarded as rituals. In this respect, the work of Turner (1969) on ritual processes represents a 'compulsory' starting point. It needs to be emphasised that in his scholarly production, Turner (1969) never made explicit the link between tourism and rituals. Rather, his work mainly concentrates on other social practices. Yet, the liminal (or liminoid) nature of the tourist experience, and the overall idea that tourism should be conceived as a *rite of passage*, has been suggested by tourism scholars.

Tanning, in a ritualistic sense, may sacredly describe the sun as a place of tribute where the celestial descends its rays upon the devotee's corporeal crusade. It involves continuous sensory chants passing through the skin until enough celestial light reaches the body to create golden crystallised skin. The ritual is repetitive and is performed with simple stylised acts. The beach, spread with silky powdery sand, is the shrine for all devotees to come in fellowship to realise this rite of passage. Before the worshipping begins, it is essential to have the whole body creamed up. When the first contact with the sun is made, the ritual is performed by lying down and subsequently being immobile, a ritual of serene aura to fully concentrate on absorbing the heat and to consciously feel the sensations produced by the sun. Occasionally, the bikini tops are left unclasped or the bottom part of the bikini purportedly pulled up to ensure full tanning success: a tanned body without visible white lines.

Urry (1990) points out that '[t]he ideal body has come to be viewed as one that is tanned' (p. 38). In many Western countries, suntan, in its narrow sense, is still closely associated with the holiday and noticeably described in tourism literature is the way tourism discourse constructs the tourist body as 'slim, tanned, young, Caucasian, female and bikinied' (Small, 2007: 87). Furthermore, as Hopwood (1995) says, for women, physical appearance signifies femininity. As such, tanning embodies a linear and progressive body transformation, which aims at a feminine idealisation. However, this ritualistic act is performative, as it plays a pivotal role in the formation of a specific tourist identity. For example, tourists on beach holidays perform patterns of behaviour that are learnt and accurately enacted to make sure they adhere to the socially constructed idealisation of *being a sun-lust tourist*. Edensor (2000: 325) points out that tourist performances and performative acts are 'enframed and informed by different discourses', namely narratives and ritualistic acts that guide and influence tourist consumption. Importantly, tourist performances are shaped by 'culturally situated symbolic meanings', which vary according to the specific spatial and socio-cultural context. Consequently, different tourist stages may produce different enactments and different levels of 'immersion' in a tourist performance (Edensor, 2000). As a case in point, the juxtaposition of the fully clothed Asian women with the scantily clad (mostly) Caucasian women as narrated against the dramatic backdrop of the blazing sun manifests contrasts of symbolic femininity in terms of complexion and corporeality. Therefore, tanning performance being influenced by spatial and socio-cultural context is both a performative act of bodily compliance and resistance to gendered performance.

If tanning, in Western contexts, is a type of feminine performative act, then sun screening could reasonably be considered to fall within the same connotation, but situated at the opposing continuum of skin tone. This performative act is stereotypically enacted by Asian women who conform to the symbolic femininity of having a fairer complexion. It is arguably sensible for most Asian women to conform to this performative act when immersed in a tanning performance, as, when heteronormative agents in society ask what personifies a woman, they are asking about certain normative conditions that must be fulfiled for a person to become one. In the theatrical sense, femininity as a gender identity is not a prop to be retained and revealed, but a prescribed set of performative acts to be made comprehensible, dramatised and well articulated to the audience. Regardless of whether it is performed effortlessly or carelessly, sensibly or haphazardly, it is nevertheless a part that must be enacted and a role that must be realised (Goffman, 1959).

As I had discovered over the years that the blazing sun was not my true companion, I did not venture far to observe the performances at the beach. I only scanned as far as my eyes could see under the shelter of my hut. The sound of rummaging through some bags next to me caused my gaze to turn away from the beach. I noticed that my travel companions had dug out a few bottles of sun-protection lotion and were prepared to start their rituals of sun screening. Armed with the highest SPF (sun protection factor) lotion, they massaged their skin delicately to ensure perfect absorption. I asked if it would be necessary to cream up, as we were well sheltered by the hut, but they claimed that we could still get tanned from the sea breeze. I questioned if it was merely a myth and they shrugged it off, as they would rather not leave anything to chance. While the girls busied themselves with their rituals, I turned towards the sea and started to let my mind wander off. Although skin colour had been generally understood as an embodiment of fixed capital, I could remember vividly seeing local and international brands advertised on television; the advertisements incessantly featured cosmetic whitening products that promised consumers of lighter and brighter skin. In fact, the symbolic value of lighter skin was so pronounced that I grew up witnessing many women in my society attempting to acquire fair-skinned privilege by using those cosmetics or other treatments to lighten their skin tone. The waves crashed against the happy swimmers in the sea and their laughter brought me back to reality. I continued to look out towards the soothing sea, but I was lost in a frothing sea of apprehension of what the true influence of skin colour on gendered performance could rightly be.

Conclusion

This chapter turns to reflexive narrative of an Asian scholar as an approach to understanding the Asian gendered performances in tourism settings, since little has been written on gender and performance within the Asian and tourism context. In order to explore the embodiment and enactment of Asian femininity, tanning performance on a beach holiday is reflexively narrated using the metaphor of theatrical performance. By reflexively narrating from the depths of my own embodied position, I have shown the significance of reflexivity and the value of embodiment in this chapter. My position as an embodied man in Asia, living and 'being there', adds credibility in understanding Asian gendered performance. I have acknowledged my critical view (contesting hegemonic masculinity in Asia) and its influence on my reflexive narration of the tanning performance of Asian and Caucasian women through this critical gendered lens. As a scholar, I feel it is important to highlight the fact that the Asia and tanning illustrated in this chapter represent a deep reflection of my own understandings in life. This specific Asian gendered performance is not a generalisation but my reflection upon specific learned experiences and observation of the people who crossed path with my own history, culture and tradition. Through reflexivity, I have narrated the importance of skin colour in Asian society, the importance of sun screening to represent Asian femininity in tourism, the patriarchal and masculinist ways of Asian society, and the femininity and skin colour with which life is lived in the Asian society that I grew up in. These narratives are important, as they contextualise my analysis in this chapter of the tanning performance and sun screening of Asian women at the beach.

In our everyday lives as social agents, we continuously 'do gender' before a set of observers. This continuous performance, which is governed by social and cultural institutions, is an act constituted in time that is stylised and repeated in order to represent gender identity (Butler, 1988). The reflexive narrative in this chapter is an illustration to highlight the fact that the attribution of femininity needs to be performed repeatedly, as being a stereotypical Asian woman is to constantly protect the symbolic skin colour that is attributed to femininity. However, from the richness of bodily practices entailed in tanning, and from the varied gender characteristics this performance embodies, tourists at the beach are perceived to deliberately and repeatedly perform their own leisurely set of bodily practices in accordance with diverse social systems and collective identities. Seeing that tanning defines the idealised body of the beach vacation in a Western context, but contradicts the symbolic femininity of being fair skinned in Asia, I suggest that tanning is both a performative act of bodily compliance and resistance to gendered performance. In this regard, from an Asian perspective, sun screening, as the antithesis of tanning, is conceived as the Asian gendered performance in tourism. Although the tanning performance reflexively narrated in this chapter suggests that there is an association between corporeality and femininity, absent from the narratives are bodies that do not conform to this feminised bodily ideal within a shared social system. As such, I propose that the narratives of this incongruence would be a valuable next step in understanding this gendered performance. Nevertheless, my reflexive narratives of tanning at the beach are embodied texts that shed light on the ways femininity as a performative act is performed and embodied in tourism, and these narratives plausibly offer a contribution to the 'empirical possibilities of an embodied account of tourism' (Johnston, 2001: 181).

References

Abramovici, M. (2007) The sensual embodiment of Italian women. In A. Pritchard, N. Morgan, I. Ateljevic and C. Harris (eds) *Tourism and Gender: Embodiment, Sensuality, and Experience* (pp. 107–125). Wallingford: CABI.

Aitchison, C. (2001) Theorizing other discourses of tourism, gender and culture: Can the subaltern speak (in tourism)? *Tourist Studies* 1 (2), 133–147.

Ateljevic, I., Harris, C., Wilson, E. and Collins, F. (2005) Getting 'entangled': Reflexivity and the 'critical turn' in tourism studies. *Tourism Recreation Research* 30 (2), 9–21.

Butler, J. (1988) Performative acts and gender constitution: An essay in phenomenology and feminist theory. *Theatre Journal* 40 (4), 519–531.

Butler, J. (2004) *Undoing Gender*. London: Routledge.

Denzin, N.K. and Lincoln, Y.S. (2011) *Handbook of Qualitative Research* (4th edn). Thousand Oaks, CA: Sage.

Doome, S. and Ateljevic, I. (2005) Tourism as a performance: Enacting backpacker tourism in Fiji. In A. Jaworski and A. Pritchard (eds) *Tourism, Discourse and Communication* (pp. 173–198). London: Routledge.

Edensor, T. (1998) *Tourists at the Taj: Performance and Meaning at a Symbolic Site*. London: Routledge.

Edensor, T. (2000) Staging tourism: Tourists as performers. *Annals of Tourism Research* 27 (2), 322–344.

Errington, S. (1990) Recasting sex, gender and power: A theoretical and regional overview. In J.M. Atkinson and S. Errington (eds) *Power and Difference: Gender in Island Southeast Asia* (pp. 1–58). Stanford, CA: Stanford University Press.

Foucault, M. (1977) *Discipline and Punish*. New York: Pantheon Books.

Geertz, C. (1973) *The Interpretation of Cultures: Selected Essays*. New York: Basic Books.

Goffman, E. (1959) *The Presentation of Self in Everyday Life*. New York: Anchor Books.

Grosz, E. (1994) *Volatile Bodies: Towards a Corporeal Feminism*. Bloomington, IN: Indiana University Press.

Hatley, B. (1990) Theatrical imagery and gender ideology in Java. In J.M. Atkinson and S. Errington (eds) *Power and Difference: Gender in Island Southeast Asia* (pp. 177–208). Stanford, CA: Stanford University Press.

Hopwood, C. (1995) My discourse/my-self: Therapy as possibility (for women who eat compulsively). *Feminist Review* 49, 66–82.

Johnston, L. (2001) (Other) Bodies and tourism studies. *Annals of Tourism Research* 28 (1), 180–201.

Richardson, L. (2000) Writing: A method of inquiry. In N.K. Denzin and Y.S. Lincoln (eds) *Handbook of Qualitative Research* (2nd edn). Thousand Oaks, CA: Sage.

Rodgers, S. (1990) The symbolic representation of women in a changing Batak culture. In J.M. Atkinson, and S. Errington (eds) *Power and Difference: Gender in Island Southeast Asia* (pp. 307–344). Stanford, CA: Stanford University Press.

Schechner, R. (1985) *Between Theater and Anthropology*. Philadelphia, PA: University of Pennsylvania Press.

Small, J. (2007) The emergence of body in the holiday accounts of women and girls. In A. Pritchard (ed.) *Tourism and Gender: Embodiment, Sensuality, and Experience* (pp. 73–91). Wallinford: CABI.

Tribe, J. (2005) New tourism research. *Tourism Recreation Research* 30 (2), 5–8.

Tsing, A.L. (1990) Gender and performance in Meratus dispute. In J.M. Atkinson and S. Errington (eds) *Power and Difference: Gender in Island Southeast Asia* (pp. 95–126). Stanford, CA: Stanford University Press.

Turner, V.W. (1969) *The Ritual Process: Structure and Anti-Structure*. London: Transaction Publishers.

Urry, J. (1990) *The Tourist Gaze: Leisure and Travel in Contemporary Societies*. London: Sage.

Veijola, S. and Jokinen, E. (1994) The body in tourism. *Theory, Culture and Society* 11, 125–151.

5 The Impact of Masculinities in the Researcher–Respondent Relationship: A Socio-Historical Perspective

Karun Rawat and Catheryn Khoo-Lattimore

Introduction

Decades after Western colonisation in Asia, many of the ideologies imparted by Western education to many Asian societies still prevail (Liu, 2011). This is consistent with the notion of the 'Eurocentric vision' that Mura and Sharif (2015) emphasised in explaining the dearth of knowledge about Asian tourism from an Asian perspective. Referring to this predicament as the 'crisis of representation', Mura and Sharif (2015) called for more researchers to 'reflect upon the political, social, cultural, historical, and institutional forces that influence tourism scholars' production and representation of research' (p. 15). A compounding rarity surrounding this crisis is the discussion of masculinities (Figueroa-Domecq et al., 2015). This is not surprising given that gender research in tourism (and the wider academy) generally comprises studies about women, their travel constraints (Aitchison et al., 1998; Bartos, 1982; Deem, 1996; di Leonardo, 1987; Harris & Ateljevic, 2003; Harris & Wilson, 2005; Heimtun, 2011; Khan, 2011; Small, 2003, 2005a, 2005b; Wilson, 2004; Wilson & Little, 2005, 2008) as well as the empowerment associated with travel (Berdychevsky et al., 2013; Butler, 1995; Green, 1998; Harris & Wilson, 2007; Henderson & Dialeschki, 1991; Jeffreys, 2003; Jordan & Gibson, 2005; Wilson & Harris, 2006). However, issues related to women's travel experiences are the consequences of the relations between women and men. Therefore, the political and sociocultural concerns with gender issues will inherently lead us to conundrums about women and men, and gender practices.

This chapter was partly inspired by the call from Mura and Sharif (2015) to close the gap on Asian scholars' reflexivity in interpretivist research but was also motivated by our own belief that the power associated with the authority of being field investigators should not to be underestimated in research (Khoo-Lattimore, 2017). In qualitative studies, where the researcher–respondent relationship is characteristically one on one, the need to reflect on the impact researchers' identities have becomes even more critical. This chapter hence aims to provide an understanding of the impact of Asian masculinities in researcher–respondent relationships from a socio-historical perspective. We present our combined reflexive considerations as two Asian academics after a study we conducted on an indigenous community in the highlands of east Malaysia. In doing so, this chapter also addresses Pritchard and Morgan's call for tourism academics 'to create a new knowledge in [the] tourism academy [by] liberat[ing] our perspective from this academic decolonisation and accept the knowledge [that] emanate[s] from Africa, Asia or from any indigenous peoples around the world' (Pritchard & Morgan, 2007: 25).

The Researcher as Research Instrument

In studies that are exploratory in nature, researchers often begin interviews with open-ended questions and require respondents to answer in an extensive manner. On the other hand, gaining access to respondents, and to respondents who will provide good, honest data, can be difficult. Poggenpoel and Myburgh (2003) warned that 'The researcher as instrument can be the greatest threat to trustworthiness in qualitative research if considerable time is not spent on preparation of the field, reflexivity of the researcher, the researcher staying humble' (p. 420). Given that the researcher is the central person collecting data from respondents in qualitative research (Denzin & Lincoln, 2000), reflection on the researcher–respondent relationship becomes even more imperative. This importance is heightened in mixed-gender researcher–respondent relationships, as social and cultural norms dictate the way men and women interact in formal and informal contexts. Knowledge and positionality are not only socially and culturally constructed but these constructions transpire over time through political agendas and are therefore also historically and culturally shaped (Hyun, 2006; Nisbett, 2003; Ormrod, 2004). This means that even before any interview encounter, the identity of the researcher would have already been formed in relation to both self and existing social constructs (Hall, 2011). Bygnes (2008) has argued that researchers need to be aware of the different power relations in the field so as to consider any likely bias that is not immediately visible. The next section details an attempt towards this awareness.

Situating the researcher in the research

In February 2014, the first author underwent a field trip to an indigenous village with about 1200 residents in east Malaysia, with the aim of exploring if and how innovative practices help to transform rural communities. The village, Bario, sits between 3200 and 6000 feet above sea level in Sarawak and is accessible via light Otter aircraft twice a day, depending on weather conditions (Adeyinka-Ojo & Khoo-Lattimore, 2013). Otherwise, the journey takes about 14 hours in a four-wheel drive or 10–12 of trekking across the forested mountains, as the quality of roads is poor apart from a logging road (Jiwan *et al.*, 2006). We were particularly interested in this community because its residents, who consist of mainly the indigenous Kelabits, have launched the e-Bario Innovation Village. This project was successful not only in introducing computers and the internet to this isolated community but it also opened e-Bario radio, which broadcasts information to residents in their local ethnic language. It is recognised as the first community radio in Malaysia and has won multiple awards.

While the second author has much secondary knowledge about Bario from a previous related project, she was never directly involved with the respondents and the community. Similarly in this project, she mentors the first author, a young Nepali male scholar, who performed the role of principal investigator. The following section will be written in the first person, as reflected by the first author, as he situates himself within his socialisation context of tourism research.

> I am a Nepali, born and raised in a middle-class family where the dream of all parents is for their son to have access to good higher education, and subsequently a respected career. This ambition of the parents, however, is not equally consistent for their daughters. Even today, in many rural areas of Nepal, females are deemed secondary to males and so access to education is still very much a privileged opportunity for boys in Nepali families. This male-focused attitude of families stems from the *arka-ko ghar janney-jaa* mentality, which perceives that any investment in a daughter's education will not garner a return because when they get married they leave their parents and are deemed to belong to their husband's family. Consequently, daughters in many households are trained from an early age to manage domestic housekeeping chores, while sons are raised and given priority access to economic resources, education and associated networks. For example, in my own family in the countryside of eastern Nepal, my aunts had to tend to the cows and cattle but my father attended school. Decades later, my sisters stayed home while I pursued my undergraduate studies in India and postgraduate studies in Malaysia.
>
> Studying in Malaysia widened my previously narrow understanding of gender and society. First, I have been raised a Hindu and come from a country that is predominantly Hindu. I am now suddenly immersed in a country where Islam is one of the main religions, alongside Buddhism. This has certainly given me a wider experience different cultures and

practices. Given the difference in religion, belief and practice, I had anticipated difficulty with my field work in Bario. However, as I sought to understand Bario and its community, I discovered that the residents and I share more similarities than differences. For one, I felt familiar in the remote landscape of Bario, which consequently also impacts on daily routines, where most of the locals are engaged in agriculture and farming as a primary occupation. Secondly, the hospitable nature, attitude and, most importantly, similar physical features of Bario residents gave me an almost immediate sense of acquaintance and of belonging to the same culture. Finally, my research led me to realise that I have a connection with my respondents not just by being a Nepali, a connection that can be traced back to the historical and political circumstances of 1963. The year is documented in Malaysian and Indonesian history as 'the Confrontation', as the two countries were at war with one another. At that time the Malaysian government sought help from the Nepalese army, which was also known then (and still is now) as the 'Gurkha army', to fight in the battle against Indonesia. Importantly, Bario was then the main base camp for the soldiers, as it sits on the border with Indonesia. The Gurkha army fostered a good relationship with the people of Bario and although the country was at war, life in Bario was peaceful, presumably due to the presence of the Gurkha army. When Sarawak gained its freedom from the British and merged into the Federation of Malaysia, the people of Bario associated their independence with the assistance, sacrifices, bravery and strength of the Gurkhas. This nuanced understanding of history has been enacted in community stories which results in what I felt as omnipresent gratitude and respect for, and trust of, Gurkhas. Unexpected to me, the masculine features of my ancestors as brave fighters have formed for my respondents an equally respected profile of me as a male, albeit researcher.

The Study

The actual field trip began in February 2015. The first author spent nine days with the indigenous community of Bario and conducted 16 interviews in total. While interviewing, participant observation was also carried out, which resulted in 12 pages or 4000 words of typed field notes. For this chapter, we conducted a reflexive analysis of the interactions between the researcher and his respondents, and explored how they have impacted on the researcher's accessibility to trustworthy data, or otherwise. We organise the reflections as two critical considerations for future scholars.

Masculinities in Asian societies

Just as Hastrup (1992) highlights, 'a researcher is positioned by her/his gender, age, "race"/ethnicity as well as by her/his biography, all of which may enable certain research method [to give] insights [within] the field' (p. 118). This means that the researcher's identity as a Nepali (Gurkha) could indeed facilitate the research process, as it tapped into the community experience with 'the Gurkha'. Our analysis of the field notes uncovered numerous points where dominant masculinities do not vary historically and culturally between the communities in Bario and Nepal. We summarise these in Table 5.1.

The observations in Table 5.1 illustrates the similar roles of gender and the somewhat rigidly defined responsibilities accorded to men and women in Kelabit and Nepalese cultures. The defined 'roles of male–female in cultures have similar implications on their work, family and ritual practice which plays a significant role in all aspects of their social life' (Lips, 2005: 117). It is evident that in the community where this study was carried out, a male is immediately associated with traditional masculine roles, such as leadership and decision-making, which almost automatically earn him sentiments of respect and hospitality. Therefore, collecting data in a community such as this could be deemed easier for a male researcher than for a female. Although the four male respondents were interested in participating in the research, the 12 female respondents were observed to be enthusiastic and cooperative, at no time cancelled or rescheduled an interview session. In addition, the male respondents tended to talk to the researcher about 'male topics', in particular the historical experience of Gurkhas with their community. Therefore, the stories from men tended to be masculine and to focus on brave men and soldiers. On the other hand, the women freely expressed their thoughts on the questions posed; conversations moved beyond patriarchal constraints and interviews with them yielded a wider range of data, covering both stories and ambitions of not just male but also of female leadership. This could have been influenced by the image of the male researcher as a Gurkha man, which for this community inadvertently affords trust and loyalty. This is therefore consistent with past findings, and confirmed that if respondents feel connected to the researcher, they are more likely to be actively involved in the discussion (Atkinson, 2002; Martin, 2001; Rigney, 1996, 1997, 1999; Smith, 2005).

Postmodern masculinities

From the social perspective of Nepali society, the positions of men and women in society began to change, albeit very slowly, during the Maoist insurgency between 1998 and 2001. War statistics revealed that 30–40% or more of Maoist cadres were women in various masculine roles, such as

Table 5.1 Similarities between cultures: The case of the Kelabit versus the Nepali

Nepali culture	Example in Kelabit culture	Impact on data collection
Decision-making		
Men are viewed as firm characters and decision-makers in the family and community	A 75-minute community meeting on 21 February 2015, at which seven men and two women were in attendance, was chaired by one of the men. In the meeting, decisions were often reached by the men and were assumed to reflect what was best for the family/community without any further discussion with and/or opposition from the two women	The view that 'a man knows best' places the male Nepali researcher in an advantageous position as an interviewer
Festival and ceremony		
At the Nepalese naming ceremony a newly born child is given a name from the family line of the father. It is customary that greater importance is attached to the naming ceremony of a male child than of a female child	On 23 February 2015, at the Bario-Asal Longhouse, a naming ceremony was observed for a male child. The feast that followed the ceremony was mainly orchestrated by the female family members in the community, who were expected to provide hospitality to all 51 invited guests	Societal preference, status and recognition are accorded to boys at an early age, and reinforced in everyday practice. The researcher was treated and received in the community as a guest who should be respectfully welcomed and accommodated, rather than a researcher whose questions could be confronting. The women who participated in the interviews were very willing to talk to the researcher on a more intimate level
Cultural practice		
It is customary that men eat first during meals and women consume meals only after the men. This notion is culturally embedded in men, especially for those who are married. This practice is widely acknowledged as an honour accorded to the men by their wives	During a local cultural performance on 27 February 2015, the queue for the buffet was headed by men. Women joined the queue only after majority of the men	The act of prioritising men and 'looking after their welfare' is believed among the women to bring them blessings. Likewise, the male researcher, whose need to gather data on the community to better understand them, was seen by the women as someone to be respected, looked after and prioritised. This could explain why the sample for this study consisted of more women (12) than men (4)

Role of women		
Women are socially and culturally expected to conduct household chores, given less decision-making power in the family and are generally suppressed within a patriarchal society	As observed from 22 to 28 February, when the interviews were conducted in different venues, married women performed dual roles, in household tasks and in farming	The performance of dual roles for the Kelabit women could be a catalyst for their responses to the interviewer, in the way they began to discuss issues of gender inequality and positionality which are rooted in our common culture

messengers, demonstration organisers and fully fledged guerilla fighters (Gautam & Koirala, 2001). At the same time, in the absence of men (who were either away at or who had perished in the war), women were forced to break the ideology of masculinity in Nepali society. Women had to undertake roles and responsibilities that were traditionally accorded to men and considered unthinkable for women, such as roofing their houses and ploughing the land. These masculine roles led women into opportunities and involvement in public space, engaging themselves with other women in labour and decision-making activities, which consequently increased their self-confidence in breaking the myth of gendered roles (Pleno, 2006; Reimer & Walter, 2013; Stronza, 2005). This level of self-confidence and participation was also seen in Kelabit women as providers of rural tourism experiences, despite the barriers and constraints faced by women in the process of becoming and being entrepreneurs (Gentry, 2007; Tucker & Boonabaana, 2012). The women who were interviewed expressed a motivation to decrease their economic dependency on their male partners and to improve their social status outside of their household chores. This ambition of the Kelabit women is also observed by other not-for-profit organisations working with the indigenous community of Bario. For example, a project leader from the World Wide Fund For Nature (WWF) Malaysia whom we interviewed later, commented:

> Women in these communities are very active and they like to get involved in the community projects and programmes and most importantly this community is receptive to new ideas. In the past, I have worked in various remote areas of Borneo; it is very difficult to find the involvement of women as 'entrepreneurs'. One of the main reasons I have observed in most of the cases, is that women are basically dominated by traditional belief of the culture and participation of men only. Secondly, men also don't like to support them. In fact, the whole community doesn't accept this change, because community and community heads themselves are

dominated by men only. This community has a practical understanding of social life; men want to involve their women. I think they realise this is an equal responsibility whether that is to do with household work or to work outside. I believe mostly, both of these activities have similar objectives to support your family either way and most importantly, in this landscape of communities, they really need to be receptive to changes and new practices.

From the interviews, Bario seems to be a good example of what Higgins-Desbiolles (2006) has highlighted – a tourism industry that is determined by its ability to shift gendered roles in its society, particularly in relation to social and cultural norms. The presence of postmodern masculinities among the Kelabit women is not only understood but recognised by the male researcher, despite his ingrained patriarchal upbringing. This is partially due to the similar socio-historical changes in gendered power shared by Kelabit and Nepali societies. Another male researcher entrenched in a strong patriarchal community may not necessarily have been able to acknowledge such findings in his research, as past studies have found that men who have had their masculinities disrupted, challenged and taken over by women felt humiliated and resorted to alcohol and narcotic consumption (Ishii, 2012). This is because gendered roles and the notion of masculinity as a male-dominated attribute has long been a mindset created to segregate the males and females according to their biological characteristics (West & Zimmerman, 1987), which is produced, practised and sustained through sophisticated cultural practice (with or by) the individual society (Thompson & Armato, 2012). As such, the socio-historical dimension of the Nepali–Kelabit dichotomy, and its impact on the positionalities of masculinities in the researcher–respondent relationship, should not be taken for granted. This socio-historical dimension in our case minimised the hierarchical gap between researcher as an 'instrument' and respondent as a 'subject' (Brannen, 1998; Cook & Fonow, 1986; Hertz, 1995; Okely, 1992) and contributed to making the interviews effective and interactive (Atkinson, 2002; Cooperative Research Centre for Aboriginal and Tropical Health, 2001; Martin, 2001; Rigney, 1996, 1997, 1999; Smith, 2005).

Conclusion

In this chapter we have explored the impact of Asian masculinities in research, specifically in data collection approaches and processes. We have done so in a reflexive manner, and considered the lived complexity of masculinity constructs in two Asian societies – that of the researcher, who is Nepali, and the other of the researched, who are Kelabit. We have demonstrated what Hall (2011) meant when he said that the researcher's identity and positionality are socially constructed even before the interview is conducted. The acquired researcher identity and its close proximity to the patriarchal society of the Kelabits helped frame a mutual relationship between the researcher and the community we were researching, and significantly contributed to the richness of data for the study. We therefore argue that encountered experiences between a community and a researcher's background play an important role during data collection, and should be considered and demarcated in the methodology section of any empirical interpretivist research.

At a time when there is a dearth of Asian researchers employing qualitative methods (Mura & Sharif, 2015), we have answered the call for tourism academics to undertake reflexive exercises throughout their research career (Khoo-Lattimore, 2017). We hope this chapter is a move forward for researchers whose work requires understanding of an unfamiliar environment and culture before immersion in the research context, but also for many scholars who need to delineate the researcher–respondent relationship in retrieving data.

References

Adeyika-Ojo, S.F. and Khoo-Lattimore, C. (2013) Slow food events as a high yield strategy for rural tourism destinations. The case of Bario, Sarawak. *Worldwide Hospitality and Tourism Themes* 5 (4), 353–364. doi:10.1108/WHATT-03-2013-0012.

Aitchison, C., Reeves, C. and Jordan, F. (1998) Gendered (bed) spaces: The culture and commerce of women only tourism. In C. Aitchison and F. Jordan (eds) *Gender, Space and Identity: Leisure, Culture and Commerce* (pp. 47–68). Brighton: Leisure Studies Association.

Atkinson, J. (2002) *Trauma Trails, Recreating Song Lines: The Transgenerational Effects of Trauma in Indigenous Australia*. North Melbourne: Spinifex Press.

Bartos, R. (1982) Women and travel. *Journal of Travel Research* 20 (4), 3–9. doi:10.1177/00472875820 2000402.

Berdychevsky, L., Gibson, H. and Poria, Y. (2013) Women sexual behaviour in tourism: Loosening the bridle. *Annals of Tourism Research* 42, 65–85. doi: 10.1016/j.annals.2013.01.006.

Brannen, J. (1988) Research note: The study of sensitive subjects. *Sociological Review* 36 (3), 552–563.

Butler, K.L. (1995) Independence for Western women through tourism. *Annals of Tourism Research* 22 (2), 487–489. doi: 10.1016/0160-7383(94)00101-4.

Bygnes, S. (2008) *Interviewing People-Oriented Elites* (Eurosphere Working Paper Series, Online Working Paper Number 10). Available at http://eurospheres.org/files/2010/08/Eurosphere_Working_Paper_10_Bygnes.pdf (accessed May 2016).

Cook, J.A. and Fonow, M.M. (1986) Knowledge and women interests: Issues of epistemology and methodology in feminist sociological research. *Sociological Inquiry* 56 (1), 2–29.

Cooperative Research Centre for Aboriginal and Tropical Health (CRCATH) (2001) *Research Partnerships: Yarning about Research with Indigenous Peoples* (Workshop Report 1). Alice Springs, Australia.

Deem, R. (1996) No time for a rest? An exploration of women work, engendered leisure and holidays. *Time and Society* 5 (1), 5–25. doi: 10.1177/0961463X96005001001.

Denzin, N.K. and Lincoln, Y.S. (eds) (2000) *Handbook of Qualitative Research* (2nd edn). Thousand Oaks, CA: Sage.

Di Leonardo, M. (1987) The female world of cards and holidays: Women, families, and the work of kinship. *Signs* 12 (3), 440-453. doi: 10.1086/494338.

Figueroa-Domecq, C., Pritchard, A., Segovia-Pérez, M., Morgan, N. and Villacé-Molinero, T. (2015) Tourism gender research: A critical accounting. *Annals of Tourism Research* 52, 87–103. doi: 10.1016/j.annals.2015.02.001.

Gautam, S. and Koirala, T. (2001) *Women and Children in the Periphery of the People's War*. Kathmandu: Institute for Human Rights Communications Nepal (IHRICON).

Gentry, K.M.K. (2007) Belizean women and tourism work: Opportunity or impediment? *Annals of Tourism Research* 34 (2), 477–496.

Green, E. (1998) 'Women doing friendship': An analysis of women leisure as a site of identity construction, empowerment and resistance. *Leisure Studies* 17 (3), 171–185. doi: 10.1080/ 026143698375114.

Hall, M. (2011) Researching the political in tourism: Where knowledge meets power. In C.M. Hall (ed.) *Fieldwork in Tourism: Methods, Issues and Reflections* (pp. 39–54). London: Routledge.

Harris, C. and Ateljevic, I. (2003) Perpetuating the male gaze as the norm: Challenges for 'her' participation in business travel. *Tourism Recreation Research* 28 (2), 21–30. doi: 10.1080/ 02508281.2003. 11081401.

Harris, C. and Wilson, E. (2005) Leaving home: Pre-travel strategies used by female business and pleasure tourists. Paper presented at the CAUTHE 2005, Sharing Tourism Knowledge, Alice Springs, Australia.

Harris, C. and Wilson, E. (2007) Travelling beyond the boundaries of constraint: Women, travel and empowerment. In A. Pritchard, N. Morgan, I. Ateljevic and C. Harris (eds) *Tourism and Gender: Embodiment, Sensuality and Experience*. Wallingford: CABI.

Hastrup, K. (1992) Writing ethnography: State of the art. In, J. Okely and H. Callaway (eds) *Anthropology and Autobiography* (pp. 115–133). London: Routledge.

Heimtun, B. (2011) The friend, the loner and the independent traveller: Norwegian midlife single women social identities when on holiday. *Gender, Place and Culture* 19 (1), 83–101. doi: 10.1080/ 0966369X.2011.617881.

Henderson, K.A. and Dialeschki, M.D. (1991) A sense of entitlement to leisure as constraint and empowerment for women. *Leisure Sciences* 13 (1), 51–65. doi: 10.1080/01490409109513124.

Hertz, R. (1995) Separate but simultaneous interviewing of husbands and wives: Making sense of their stories. *Qualitative Inquiry* 1 (4), 429–451.

Higgins-Desbiolles, F. (2006) More than an industry: The forgotten power of tourism as a social force. *Tourism Management* 27 (6), 1192–1208.

Hyun, E. (2006) *Teachable Moments: Re-conceptualizing Curricula Understandings (Studies in the Postmodern Theory of Education)*. New York: Peter Lang.

Ishii, K. (2012) The impact of ethnic tourism on hill tribes in Thailand. *Annals of Tourism Research* 39 (1), 290–310.

Jeffreys, S. (2003) Sex tourism: Do women do it too? *Leisure Studies* 22 (3), 223–238. doi: 10.1080/ 0261436032000075452.

Jiwan, D., Paul, C.P.K., Teo, G.K. and Jiwan, M. (2006) Integrated highland development in Bario, Sarawak, Malaysia: An overview. Paper presented at the International Symposium Towards Sustainable Livelihoods and Ecosystems in Mountainous Regions, Chiang Mai, 7–9 March.

Jordan, F. and Gibson, H. (2005) 'We're not stupid ... But we'll not stay home either': Experiences of solo women travelers. *Tourism Review International* 9 (2), 195–211. doi: 10.3727/15442720 5774791663.

Khan, S. (2011) Gendered leisure: Are women more constrained in travel for leisure? *Tourismos* 6 (1), 105–121.

Khoo-Lattimore, C. (2017) The ethics of excellence in tourism research: A reflexive analysis and implications for early career researchers. *Tourism Analysis*, forthcoming.

Lips, H.M. (2005) *Sex and Gender: An Introduction* (5th edn). New York: McGraw-Hill.

Liu, J.H. (2011) Asian epistemologies and contemporary social psychological research. In N.K. Denzin and Y.S. Lincoln (eds) *The Sage Handbook of Qualitative Research* (4th edn) (pp. 213–226). Thousand Oaks, CA: Sage.

Martin, K. (2001) Ways of knowing, ways of being and ways of doing: Developing a theoretical framework and methods for indigenous research and indigenist research. Paper presented at the AIATSIS Indigenous Studies Conference, 'The Power of Knowledge, The Resonance of Tradition', Australian National University, Canberra.

Mura, P. and Sharif, S.P. (2015) The crisis of the 'crisis of representation' – mapping qualitative tourism research in Southeast Asia. *Current Issues in Tourism* 18 (9). doi: 10.1080/13683500.2015.1045459.

Nisbett, R.E. (ed.) (2003) *The Geography of Thought: How Asians and Westerners Think Differently and Why*. New York: Free Press.

Okely, J. (1992) Anthropology and autobiography: Participatory experience and embodied knowledge. In J. Okely and H. Callaway (eds) *Anthropology and Autobiography* (pp. 1–28). London: Routledge.

Ormrod, J.E. (ed.) (2004) *Human Learning* (4th edn). Upper Saddle River, NJ: Pearson.

Pleno, M.J.L. (2006) Ecotourism projects and women empowerment: A case study in the province of Bohol, Philippines. *Forum of International Development Studies* 32, 137–154.

Poggenpoel, M. and Myburgh, S. (2003) The researcher as research instrument in educational research: A possible threat to trustworthiness? *Education* 124 (2), 418–421.

Pritchard, A. and Morgan, N. (2007) De-centering tourism's intellectual universe or the dialectic between change and tradition. In I. Ateljevic, A. Pritchard and N. Morgan (eds) *The Critical Turn in Tourism Studies* (pp. 12–28). Oxford: Elsevier.

Reimer, J.K. and Walter, P. (2013) How do you know it when you see it? Community-based ecotourism in the Cardamom Mountains of Southwestern Cambodia. *Tourism Management* 34, 122–132.

Rigney, L.I. (1996) Tools for an indigenist research methodology: A Narungga perspective. Paper presented at the World Indigenous Peoples Conference: Education, Albuquerque, New Mexico.

Rigney, L.I. (1997) Internationalisation of an indigenous anti-colonial cultural critique of research methodologies: A guide to indigenist research methodology and its principles. Paper presented at the Higher Education Research and Development Society of Research Australia (HERSDA) Annual International Conference, 'Research and Development in Higher Education: Advancing International Perspectives', Adelaide, South Australia.

Rigney, L.I. (1999) The first perspective: Culturally safe research practices on or with indigenous peoples. Keynote address at the Chacmool Conference, University of Calgary, Alberta, Canada.

Small, J. (2003) The voices of older women tourists. *Tourism Recreation Research* 28 (2), 31–39. doi: 10.1080/02508281.2003.11081402.

Small, J. (2005a) Women holidays: Disruption of the motherhood myth. *Tourism Review International* 9 (2), 139–154. doi: 10.3727/154427205774791645.

Small, J. (2005b) Holiday experiences of women and girls over the life-course. Doctoral dissertation, University of Technology, Sydney, Australia. Available at https://opus.lib.uts.edu.au/handle/10453/28053 (accessed May 2016).

Smith, L.T. (2005) *Decolonizing Methodologies: Research and Indigenous peoples*. London: Zed Books.

Stronza, A. (2005) Hosts and hosts: The anthropology of community-based ecotourism in the Peruvian Amazon. *National Association for Practice of Anthropology Bulletin* 23, 170–190.

Thompson, M.E. and Armato, M. (2012) *Investigating Gender*. Cambridge: Polity Press.

Tucker, H. and Boonabaana, B. (2012) A critical analysis of tourism, gender and poverty reduction. *Journal of Sustainable Tourism* 20 (3), 437–455.

West, C. and Zimmerman, D.H. (1987) Doing gender. *Gender and Society* 1 (2), 125–151.

Wilson, E. (2004) A 'journey of her own?': The impact of constraints on women solo travel. Doctoral dissertation, Griffith University, Brisbane, Australia). https://www120.secure.griffith.edu.au/rch/items/4b2568ae-3516-05f7-bbc7-3acd31f17b1c/1 (accessed May 2016).

Wilson, E. and Harris, C. (2006) Meaningful travel: Women, independent travel and the search for self and meaning. *Tourism* 54 (2), 161–172.

Wilson, E. and Little, D.E. (2005) A 'relative escape'? The impact of constraints on women who travel solo. *Tourism Review International* 9 (2), 155–175. doi: 10.3727/154427205774791672.

Wilson, E. and Little, D.E. (2008) The solo female travel experience: Exploring the 'geography of women fear'. *Current Issues in Tourism* 11 (2), 167–186. doi: 10.2167/cit342.0.

6 The Asian Female Tourist Gaze: A Conceptual Framework

Eunice Tan and Barkathunnisha Abu Bakar

Introduction

The current dynamic economic climate and socio-demographic developments in Asia have had a significant impact on international tourism trends in recent years. With the rapid expansion and transformation of Asian economies, the phenomenon of the 'Asian wave' has altered the face of tourism and hospitality in this Asian century, both within and beyond the Asia Pacific region (Leung *et al.*, 2011; Winter, 2009). Asian travellers have developed a strong desire to travel to the West to see and experience these places and people that appear to have defined global cultures. Despite this awareness and criticisms by many academics (Gladstone, 2006; Winter, 2009), most tourism studies have taken an ethnocentric perspective, taking Western travellers as their empirical starting point (Tribe, 2001). To date, the bulk of research has been preoccupied with Western forms of tourism and their social, cultural and economic impacts on communities, places and environments (Winter, 2009).

Concurrently, today's international outbound tourism market has witnessed the brisk growth of the female traveller segment (Kim *et al.*, 2012; Zhang & Hitchcock, 2014). Female travellers currently comprise 50% of the world's leisure travel population (Li *et al.*, 2011) and have become the primary target market for many tourism businesses. Globally, women play a significant role in tourism, as visitors, hosts and employees in the tourism sector. Women are travel influencers and are increasingly gaining importance in travel consumption. Female travellers possess strong purchasing power and demonstrate a greater intent than their male counterparts to spend more at tourism destinations (Chan, 2007; Kim & Beck, 2009). However, despite this growth, Remoaldo *et al.* (2014) observe that while gender-based and feminist research is well established in the humanities and social sciences, the investigation of gender in tourism has been limited and has received very little empirical attention. Westwood *et al.* (2000: 353) argue that

> ... the reluctance of many tourism writers and practitioners to recognise gender-specific concerns and to fully incorporate gender awareness ... has led to gender blindness and thus consumer dissatisfaction. As women travellers hold different attitudes, expectations, perceptions of tourism experiences, a deeper understanding of female consumers will have valuable implications for tourism.

Thus, in this chapter we endeavour to present the emic voices of the Asian female tourist, specifically, interpreted from a Singaporean perspective. We aim to highlight the kaleidoscope of cultural- and gender-based elements that constitute the Asian female gaze, and dispel misconceptions and overgeneralisation of the universal tourist gaze. In writing this chapter, we as researchers have combined academic discourse with our own personal narratives to investigate the 'state of mind' of Asian female travellers (Noy, 2007: 349). Through a critical reflection of our varied travel experiences as leisure travellers, and our inner dialogues, we have voiced the lives, experiences and worldviews that have influenced the experiences of the subjects we are researching. A methodological proposition in the form of autoethnography is set out to help us delve into our lived experiences as Singaporean female tourists. A non-traditional research method is necessary to examine and communicate the cognitive, affective and spiritual dimension of our travel experiences in ways that are not purely academic and cerebral. In this study, our voices and positionality as Asian females provide a more insightful and deeper approach to a subject matter that has been inadequately examined through a Eurocentric male lens.

From our literature research, we have found few studies undertaken by Asian academics on the contemporary Asian female traveller. Current research on socio-cultural issues pertaining to the Asian tourist undertaken by Western researchers may be inadequate in grasping the Asian mindset (Pearce *et al.*, 2013; Winter, 2009). While there have been studies undertaken in recent years on the contemporary Asian tourist (Assiouras *et al.*, 2015; Kim & Lee, 2000; Prayang *et al.*, 2015; Wong, 2013; Yang & Wu, 2014) and female travellers (Kim & Beck, 2009; Khoo-Lattimore & Prayag, 2015; Pritchard & Morgan, 2000; Sun & Qu, 2011; Westwood *et al.*, 2000), there has been limited investigation specifically of the Asian female tourist (Asbollah *et al.*, 2013; Cai & Combrink, 2000; Chan, 2007; Kim *et al.*, 2012; Li *et al.*, 2011; Zhang & Hitchcock, 2014). Therefore, this chapter will explore the determinants of gender and culture on Urry's (1992) broad concept of the tourist gaze using an interpretive autoethnographic approach. It builds upon the gender and cultural paradigm of the tourist gaze (Urry & Larsen, 2011) and seeks to discover how these gazes are constructed and performed during the travel experiences of Asian female travellers. This chapter will introduce a conceptual model to examine the Asian female gaze in tourism settings and contribute to a larger, expanding corpus of work examining gender, culture and tourist gaze in the contemporary globalised world.

The Tourist Gaze

Urry (1990) applied Foucault's (1994) conceptual architecture of *le regard* or 'the gaze' to tourism experiences to explore the implications of the various forms of gazes for the tourist self and tourism setting (Bruner, 1991; Maoz, 2006; Pritchard & Morgan, 2000). As most tourism experiences involve sightseeing, and are all about 'seeing and being seen' (Jenkins, 2000), there is an emphasis on the significance of seeing and the collection of sights. The social practices of tourism are closely connected to vision and an all-seeing eye. Tourists perceive and interpret the world through their socially influenced and personally developed lenses (Pearce *et al.*, 2013). Essentially, the gaze is 'what is in a tourist's mindset ... what they see, are aware of, expect and are conscious of' (Buddhabhumbhitak, 2010: 141). Urry (1990) describes tourists' experiences in destinations as signs or markers that are visually different from their everyday life and experiences. The gaze consumes the markers of the tourist space, which frames the tourist's experiences and bestows importance and meaning to these experiences. The tourist gaze can be classified as romantic gaze or collective gaze. The former places importance on solitude, privacy and a personal relationship with the object of the gaze, while the latter stresses the need for the collective presence of other tourists for the success of tourism places and experiences (Urry, 1992). Many tourism studies have explored tourists' tendencies to see destinations as liminal spaces (Ryan & Hall, 2001) and the tendency for the tourist gaze to exocitise or eroticise spaces toured (Pritchard & Morgan, 2000; Shepherd, 2009). The traveller together with the residents and workers at the places toured form mutually gazing tourism encounters during the liminal state.

However, many researchers have critiqued the use of Urry's (1990) initial notion of tourist gaze in tourism research as being overly Eurocentric, as well as its uncritical application to Asian tourists and tourism (Asbollah *et al.*, 2013; Maoz, 2006; Winter, 2009; Zhang & Hitchcock, 2014). The tourist gaze as a concept stemmed from leisure experiences in an industrialising Europe, but the term has been universally applied where 'the tourist' is conceived as a singular subject that is white and male (Winter, 2009). There has been an accepted norm in tourism discourse in gazing on Western tourists as a globally recognisable subject and in applying analytical and theoretical approaches. While globalisation has brought about reconfigurations of and new perspectives on the single tourist gaze of the 19th century, despite these changes, little attention has been given to regional, cultural and geographical differences, and non-Western forms of leisure travel have been ignored in mainstream discourse and theories about tourism. Urry (2001) himself acknowledged the multiple gazes that have surfaced from the single gaze of the 19th century, due to the awakening of global culture leading to the 'proliferation of countless discourses, forms and embodiments' of tourist gazes in the postmodern era (Urry, 2001: 7). The major global shifts necessitate a pluralistic perspective and a need to relook at the universalisms at the core of tourism studies (Winter, 2009). The exponential growth in Asian tourism and the wider societal implications arising out of this development require a reorientation of how tourism is researched and understood.

The Asian Female Gaze: Influence of Cultural and Gender Identity

With the globalisation of tourism markets and the current social, cultural and economic shift towards the Asian tourist, research that concentrates on understanding the socio-cultural aspects of tourist behaviour and decision-making from an Asian-centric perspective becomes all the more vital. To enable a better grasp and interpretation of the Asian tourism phenomenon, it is useful first to understand Asian cultural values, their evolution and where they come from (Assiouras et al., 2015; Kim & Lee, 2000; Mok & Defranco, 2000; Winter, 2009; Wong, 2013). This is critical, considering the vastly heterogeneous characteristics of Asian societies, cultures and populations. These differences and their impacts on tourism and consumption patterns have been well discussed by a number of authors (Assiouras et al., 2015; Kim & Lee, 2000; Mok & Defranco, 2000; Pearce et al., 2013). Understanding a particular culture should not merely be concerned with a society's artifacts or performances, but should also include its values, ideologies, mindset and symbolic meanings.

Hofstede (1980) explains that culture is fundamentally the collective programming of the mind, in which cultural patterns exhibited by individuals are deeply rooted within the value systems of particular societies and community groups. These values constitute the basis through which culturally predisposed knowledge is accumulated and expressed (Li & Cai, 2012). The differences in cultural values and mindset serve to guide and influence the attitudes, beliefs and behaviour of tourists originating from varied destinations, manifesting as diverse facets of tourist behaviour and consumption patterns (Asbollah et al., 2013; Kim & Lee, 2000; Meng, 2010; Tsang, 2011). Tsang and Ap (2007) observe significant cultural differences between Asian and Western tourists' perceptions of tourism experiences and hospitality service quality while travelling. For example, it was found that while Westerners may value efficiency, time savings and goal achievement, Asian visitors would often perceive the quality of interpersonal relationships and interactions as a critical factor.

Hofstede's (1980) widely cited study of national cultures explores variances in values and behaviours across different nationalities within the dimensions of (1) power distance, (2) individualism and collectivism, (3) masculinity and femininity, and (4) uncertainty avoidance. Compared with the individualistic cultures of Western tourists, Asian tourists generally exhibit collectivistic behaviours and socio-cultural norms. For example, Asian societies commonly emphasise collaboration, shared responsibility, tolerance, social harmony, communal courtesy, group compliance and moral discipline as the cornerstones of a civilised society (Hofstede, 2001).

Linkages to social reference groups not only elucidate and govern familial and interpersonal relationships, but also shape the collective gaze and cultural lenses through which knowledge, meanings and experiences are constructed. Pearce *et al.*'s (2013) study of Chinese tourists highlights the convergence of cultural and social influences on an individual's behaviour, based on affiliations with the notions of Confucianism, patriarchalism, Buddhism and familial bonds. Such ideology and respect for affiliated traditions shape the social behaviours and interactions of Chinese tourists while travelling. Although it is acknowledged that certain social behaviours (e.g. being friendly, honest, sincere, polite and respectful) are commonly expected in most social situations across different cultures, there are cultural differences in gestures, facial expressions, civility and graciousness (Reisinger & Turner, 2002). Pearce *et al.* (2013) highlight Chinese tourists' affinity to group tours, and found that beyond the practical aspects of group-based packaged travel (e.g. economical value, language and convenience), there is also a strong desire to be with other Chinese travellers while touring. These tourists' social needs and behaviours stem from the central role that family and friends traditionally play in everyday life. Even while travelling, this in-group affiliation and connectedness with others from a similar sociocultural background are conscientiously sought and enjoyed.

Mok and Defranco (2000) posit that individuals of Chinese ethnic origin (from within and outside China) have cultural values and traits related to (1) interdependence – e.g. reciprocity, appreciation, honour and friendship; (2) group orientation – e.g. kinship and *guanxi*; (3) face – e.g. respect, prestige and avoidance of criticism or embarrassment; (4) harmony – e.g. complaint and conflict avoidance; (5) respect for authority – e.g. hierarchical norms, respecting the opinions of seniors, social etiquette and protocols; and (6) external attribution – e.g. fate, superstition and taboos. The authors observe that these individuals commonly exhibit a fundamental supposition that a person's existence is tied to their mutual and complementary relationships with others. This socially constructed notion of harmonisation and maintenance of consideration for others is also observed in other Asian cultures and societies. Kim and Lee (2000) discuss the cultural differences between Anglo-American and Japanese tourists, and observe that while Anglo-American tourists exhibit individualistic characteristics in expressing travel motives, Japanese tourists exhibit collectivistic traits and a propensity to family integrity, healthy interpersonal relationships, social-emotional interdependence, and prestige/status. Therefore, a thorough insight into the cultural and value differences between Western and Asian tourist segments can provide an in-depth understanding of their attitudinal and behavioural responses to different tourism experiences.

The Asian Female Gaze and the Consumption of Tourism Spaces

Space and place in tourism settings are social and cultural constructions rather than physical locations and have no objective reality (Shurmer-Smith & Hannam, 1994). The tourist gaze of a place is socially constructed by the tourists themselves (Hollinshead, 1999) and, thus, it is imperative to consider how places are perceived and contextualised by tourists through their gaze. In discussing the intersubjective realities of tourism places, Shields (1991) highlights the need to explore the 'emotional geography' of spaces, where 'power, identity, meaning and behaviour are constructed, negotiated and renegotiated according to socio-cultural dynamics' (p. 6). Gender is critical to the social construction, as tourism spaces and places are 'both shaped by, and is a shaper of, gender in a gender–space dialectic' (Aitchison *et al.*, 1998: 51). Similarly, Kinnaird and Hall (1994: 5) explain that, as tourism is a process constructed out of gendered societies, 'all aspects of tourism-related development and activity embody gender relations'. An individual's view of herself/himself and the world around them is socially contrived and driven by gender orientation (Kim *et al.*, 2007).

Sun and Qu (2011) posit that the divergence in attitudinal and behavioural responses between genders could be significantly entrenched within biological factors. These biological factors (e.g. hormones, brain structure and thought processes) can explain the differences between women and men in terms of personalities, proclivities, emotions and moods when interpreting environmental stimuli. There is also a need to consider the social-psychological factors that influence situational processes, since individuals think and act differently according to their perceptions of their gender roles and social expectations. Gender is a fundamental part of our core identity, which is experienced in self-awareness and behaviour, derived through socially constructed roles and relationships, values, attitudes, behaviours and personality traits (Jucan & Jucan, 2013). Thus, by reviewing gender as collectively embedded constructs in social interactions, we can have a better understanding of the way women and men approach tourism experiences, and their interactions with local hosts and other travellers (Remoaldo et al., 2014). Zhang and Hitchcock (2014) further suggest that female tourist behaviour is often affected not only by the social and cultural constructs of the destination being visited, but also women's own established notions of what embodies proper female behaviour. Female travellers differ significantly from their male counterparts in terms of their travel behaviour and motivations, destinations sought and preferred tourism experiences (Kim & Beck, 2009; Kim et al., 2007; Li et al., 2011; Sun & Qu, 2011; Westwood et al., 2000; Wong, 2013). Thus, segmenting tourist markets along gender lines may be a strategic approach to meet the needs of potential international tourists, since marketing messages communicated are more effective if delivered in a manner that addresses the respective behavioural and cognitive qualities of male and female travellers (Kim et al., 2012; Sun & Qu, 2011).

However, the gendered nature of tourist motivations and tourism experience as well as gendered relations in tourism have been poorly researched and are poorly understood (Kinnaird & Hall, 1996). Hall et al. (2003) observe that, to date, there has been relatively little engagement between feminist studies and tourism studies in the progress of gender thinking in tourism. Pritchard and Morgan (2000) argue that tourism landscapes, which are gendered, appeal to the male heterosexual gaze, and that the language and imagery of tourism promotion are predominantly male-dominated, and peripheralise women's needs and desires. As discussed above, there are differences in the way women and men are involved in the consumption and construction of tourism, and studies have highlighted the differences in male and female tourism experiences (Humberstone & Collins, 1998; Jucan & Jucan, 2013; Kim & Beck, 2009; Wearing & Wearing, 1996). However, there is a general tendency to assume that male appeals are universal. By privileging the male gaze, tourism promotion and communications evidently ignore the diversity of the tourism market and the increasing role of female consumers in travel decision-making and society. A narrow focus on the male gaze in tourism studies blinds researchers to the gendered complexities of contemporary tourism and the power relations that it encompasses (Pritchard & Morgan, 2000). It is also too simplistic to portray the 'master subject' in tourism processes and settings as 'white, male, heterosexual, and bourgeois' (Anderson, 1996: 198). When tourism landscapes are gendered in favour of the male norm, tourism discourses can dangerously reflect, reinforce and affirm gender and international power relations, and inequalities among genders, races and nations (Pritchard & Morgan, 2000), where the male traveller from the West is privileged over females and those from the developing world. As highlighted by Denzin (1995: 217), 'the feminine ... and ethnic gaze ... hears and sees things that escape the white, masculine eye', and when given the opportunity will present different versions of reality and challenge existing norms. Therefore, there is a need to present new insights and perspectives in tourism that will appeal to a variety of gazes and displace the polarising male, heterosexist gaze. We need to acknowledge the gendered complexities of tourism, as all parts of the tourism experience are affected by our shared understanding of the social construction of gender.

Asian Gender-Based Studies: The Need for Reflexivity

We set out on this chapter with the aim of undertaking an exploratory study of the Asian female tourist gaze from a socio-cultural perspective. The chapter's research design was thus grounded on a post-positivist paradigm to produce interpretive and reflective narratives of tourist behaviours (Riley & Love, 2000; Tribe, 2001). Hughes (1990) and Denzin and Lincoln (1994) argue in favour of a qualitative interpretive approach since the social experiences of the researched can be understood by capturing their inner meanings. In addition, researchers have promoted reflexive vistas in the interpretation of tourist behaviours whereby the researcher's values, experiences, beliefs and social identities are involved in the construction of the research knowledge (Denzin & Lincoln, 2000). Tourism research is gradually reaching a mature stage (Pernecky, 2007) and a critical turn (Ateljevic *et al.*, 2005) where innovative methods of academic enquiry are encouraged and accepted. Tourism studies are seeing the beginning of a qualitative makeover and there have been some notable studies on the gendered nature of tourism experiences that employ social constructionist, feminist and interpretive qualitative paradigms (McCabe, 2003). These approaches are mainly undertaken with the aim of challenging white, male, Eurocentric philosophical research practices (referred to as 'phallocentric' and 'malestream' research) that are grounded on positivism (Heimtun & Morgan, 2012: 289). Standpoint feminists challenge the belief that women and men do research in the same ways and argue that quantification in a positivist paradigm is a 'smokescreen for male privilege' (Hughes & Cohen, 2012: 2). They propose that qualitative enquiry can generate understanding of women's lived experiences.

Alatas (2006) recommends a more humanistic, qualitative and value-driven research in tourism studies as an alternative discourse and to steer away from Eurocentrism. In the current critical tourism phase, researchers are venturing into reflexive and critical forms of academic enquiry in ethnographic research (Anderson, 2006), exploring the meaning behind data and seeking to understand the complexities surrounding the tourism phenomenon. In tourism scholarship there has been inadequate attention given to the personal voice of either the subject or the researcher (Swain, 1995). Particularly in the study of gender in tourism, researcher reflexivity and qualitative research approaches are important to pursue, as they increase the relevance of current research to the varied global audience and stakeholders with whom researchers need to communicate (Ellis & Bochner, 2000). Autoethnography is an approach where the researcher analyses his/her personal experiences (auto), in the process of understanding cultural experiences (ethno). This method recognises the influences of researchers' personal experiences and allows for, and accepts, subjectivity and emotionality instead of assuming that they do not exist (Ellis et al., 2011). The goal of autoethnography is to seek, recognise and utilise subjective experience as an inherent part of research, as it provides 'insider meanings' (Anderson, 2006: 389). The researcher's personal experiences and feelings are deemed significant data for understanding the social world that is being studied. When researchers undertake autoethnography, they use methodological tools and research literature to analyse their experiences, and also use their personal experiences to explain aspects of the cultural experience being investigated to facilitate understanding for insiders and outsiders (Ellis et al., 2011).

Autoethnographic enquiry advocates the heuristic investigation and reflexivity of an author's own experiences within the researched phenomenon to facilitate representational richness and contextual understanding (Canton & Santos, 2007; Humphreys, 2005). Specifically within the context of this study, reflexive/narrative ethnography is adopted – i.e. using a narrative approach (Ellis & Bochner, 2000), in which we, as researchers and fellow Asian female travellers, include our own personal, reflexive stories and perspectives within the narratives. In doing so, layered accounts are provided, that focus on our own experiences combined with data and appropriate literature. Accordingly, we set out to explore our own *memories of experiences* (Canton & Santos, 2007) as female Asian tourists during our travels. Before embarking on that section of the chapter, we brainstorm and share with each other our myriad of tourism encounters and experiences, allowing us to create a list of memorable and meaningful experiences which we feel relate to the present study and its associated considerations. These *autoethnographic vignettes* (Humphreys, 2005) are then reviewed and compared with the factors outlined in our conceptual framework. From there we select the ones from which we feel best capture the sensitivities, sensibilities and evocation of the Asian female tourist experiential journey. Here, data collection and analyses occur concurrently and existing research is compared and questioned against our own experiences. These layered accounts use reflexivity, introspection, vignettes and multiple voices to invite the audience to enter into the 'emergent experience' of doing and writing research (Ronai, 1992: 123).

Conceptual Framework

Based on the literature and current discourse, we believe that there is a need for an alternative view of the tourist gaze to adequately understand

and interpret the phenomenon of contemporary Asian female travel. The following conceptual framework (Figure 6.1) is proposed, in which the Asian female tourist gaze is affected by an amalgamation of self-directed dimensions (i.e. antecedent and self-identity factors) and other-directed dimensions (i.e. situational and interpersonal factors). These dimensions are inherent in the way that we consume markers of the tourist space, which in turn shapes our experiences and bestows importance and socially constructed meaning on our tourism encounters (Buddhabhumbhitak, 2010; Urry, 1990). These two dimensions consequently affect our cognitive (mind) and emotional (heart) reflexivity; and physical (body) and spiritual (soul) being. This process of meaning-making ultimately determines the reflective and interpretive experiences of tourism consumption, through which there are specific emotional, cognitive and behavioural outcomes. As highlighted by Pearce et al. (2013), a person's tourism experience is an accumulation of their cognitive, affective, sensory, behavioural and relationship dimensions. Additionally, Ali (2012) posits the significance of one's cultural identity and notions of the self, based on the dynamics of ethnic, religious and racial identity. These gendered and culturally affected standpoints and interpretations provide valuable information through which the Asian female gaze can be understood (Asbollah et al., 2013).

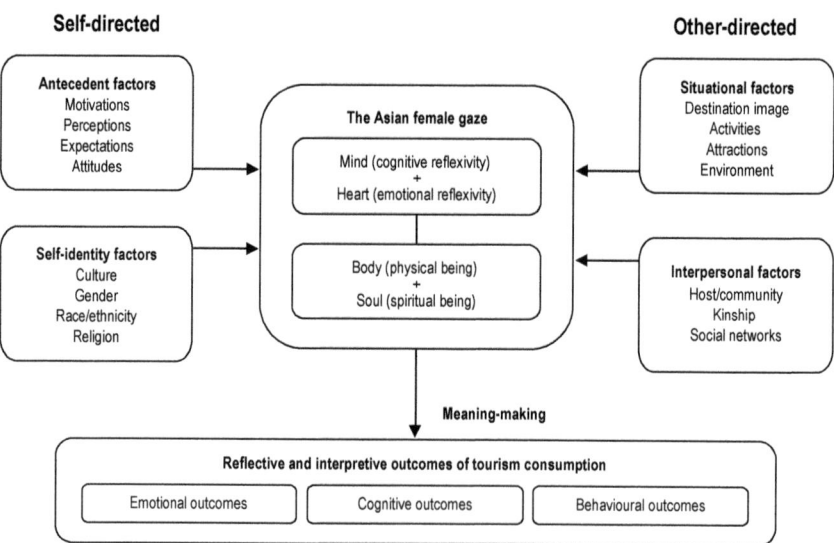

Figure 6.1 Conceptual framework for the Asian female tourist gaze

The Asian Female Tourist Gaze: Reflexivity Through Culturally Tinted Lenses

In this section of the chapter we review the cultural, social and behavioural dimensions of the Asian female tourist gaze, based upon the inherent dimensions outlined in the conceptual framework. Specifically, Singapore is used as the context from which we investigate the core themes within this study. While we may have from different ethnic origins and religious backgrounds, we intrinsically still consider ourselves as Singaporeans first. Our shared social and cultural constructions thus offer similarities in our perceptions, meanings and experiences as Asian female tourists. Our own *autoethnographic vignettes* and *memories of experiences* shared will be supported with data obtained from the dimensions of cultural orientation investigated in a study by Transnational Management Associates Ltd (TMA, 2015).

Singaporean cultural values and orientation

TMA provides training solutions to organisations to develop talents in a global workforce. The company helps organisations understand and become aware of their culturally diverse landscape and appreciate how cultural orientations affect people's attitudes and actions. TMA developed the *Worldprism*, a practical tool for developing cultural intelligence in organisations and *Country Navigators*, a source that compiles and provides in-depth, country-specific information on the cultural profiles of more than 50 countries. Within that context, cultural intelligence is the ability to recognise different cultural orientations as well as the knowledge and skills to work across such orientations effectively. Although the tool was developed for business settings, the findings on the different cultural orientations are transferable and can be applied to various cross-cultural settings, including tourism. TMA (2015) proposes three dimensions to evaluate people's cultural orientations: (1) relating – how we interact; (2) regulating – how we manage; and (3) reasoning – how we think (Table 6.1). The *Country Navigator* presents the cultural profile of Singaporeans along these three dimensions of cultural orientation, in relation to three other key Asian markets (namely, China, India and Japan) (Table 6.2).

These cultural orientations become the lenses through which we interpret, give meaning and experience the markers of the outer world. The above cultural orientations serve as a platform from which we, as female Asian tourists, explore our own *memories of experiences*. These *autoethnographic vignettes* will be narrated through the four themes within the conceptual framework presented above: (1) emotional reflexivity, (2) cognitive reflexivity, (3) physical being and (4) spiritual being.

Table 6.1 Dimensions of cultural orientation

Dimension	Characterisation	
Dimension 1: Relating – Expectations of how to interact appropriately with others	*Task-oriented* Impersonal – rules before relationships	*Relationship-oriented* Personal – Relationships before rules
	Explicit Meaning is stated directly	*Implicit* Meaning often has to be inferred from what is said and not said; and body language
	Individual-oriented 'Me before we'	*Group-oriented* 'We before me'
Dimension 2: Regulating – Expectations of how to manage our work together	*Risk-taking* Making change happen; acting decisively New is good	*Risk-avoiding* Avoiding change; Steady, but sure Stress continuity
	Tight Being punctual, controlling time. Time is money	*Loose* Being flexible, going with the flow Things will happen in their own time
	Shared Distributing power and authority within the group	*Concentrated* Focusing power and authority on specific people in the group
Dimension 3: Reasoning – Expectations of how to think about problems and present solutions	*Linear* Analytical, step-by-step process toward solution	*Circular* Focusing on exploring and integrating perspectives in a relatively unstructured way.
	Facts Emphasis on data and concrete experiences	*Thinking* Emphasis on reasoning, concepts, and logic
	Simple Focuses on essentials with little context	*Complex* Focuses on developing a detailed, contextual understanding

Emotional reflexivity

Although Singaporeans may seem very Westernised, task-oriented and highly conversant in English, intrinsically we have a strong Asian cultural heritage. We generally hold a firm respect for our cultural roots (the majority of Singaporeans are Chinese, Malay or Indian; and other minority ethnicities); and these common core Asian values bind us together as fellow

Table 6.2 Scale positions of cultural orientation based on country of origin and profile

	China	India	Japan	Singapore	
1. Relating – How I relate to others					
Task (1)	10	8	6	7	Relationship (10)
Explicit (1)	8	7	10	8	Implicit (10)
Individual (1)	9	7	10	8	Group (10)
2. Regulating – How I make decisions					
Risk-taking (1)	9	9	8	6	Risk-avoiding (10)
Tight (1)	8	9	1	3	Loose (10)
Shared (1)	9	8	8	9	Concentrated (10)
3. Reasoning – How I think					
Linear (1)	7	7	7	6	Circular (10)
Facts (1)	10	9	3	4	Thinking (10)
Simple (1)	8	8	7	7	Complex (10)

Source: TMA (2015)

Singaporeans (e.g. consensus-building, community and family focus over self). In considering familial connections, Nisha reflects:

> Travel to me is an escape from the stresses of work. But it is also a time for family bonding and spending quality time with loved ones. I plan activities and experiences that provide me with the opportunity to connect with the family and make up for the loss of moments back home.

Zhang and Hitchcock (2014) observe that Chinese women also view vacations as more than a leisure pursuit, as one that facilitates family bonding and enables them to fulfil their traditional and familial obligations. Similarly, Singapore's ethnic communities traditionally exhibit a strong group and relationship focus, wherein relationships still play a prevailing role in interpersonal interactions. Trust, respect and relationships are usually established over a long period of time. The socialisation process to get to know another party is highly valued and emphasised, wherein *guanxi* and connections built on trust and reciprocity are prevalent. An example of this is revealed by Eunice:

> When travelling, it is common that we will conscientiously shop for unique gifts and souvenirs from the destination being visited for families,

friends and others in our social network. Often these gifts brought back from our travels signify a token of our endearments, and that they were in our thoughts while we were away.

This propensity for gift-giving is similarly observed in Pearce et al.'s (2013) study of Chinese tourists, wherein gift-giving is a common, socially driven behaviour and viewed as symbolically important when returning to social and familial groups after a time away. Similarly, Mok and Defranco (2000) relate such gift-giving as important symbols of friendship, appreciation, courtesy and respect within interpersonal relations.

Singlish (colloquial English infused with elements of Chinese, Malay and Tamil) is a commonly used form of communication and is enjoyed (even proudly embraced) by many Singaporeans as our own unique brand of language, bringing together our melting pot of diverse cultures and ethnicities. While we may speak fluent and 'proper' English within formal or professional contexts, it is not uncommon for us to break into Singlish when conversing with family, friends or fellow Singaporeans in informal settings. This shared colloquial linguistic style offers a familiar cultural and social environment, from which we establish a strong group affinity almost instantaneously. Nisha shares, 'while being in an unfamiliar environment, the sound of a fellow traveller uttering Singlish brings a certain affiliation, interaction and often friendship with the fellow Singaporean, a familiar stranger'. This is also observed among Chinese tourists who forge new friendships with other Chinese travellers whom they meet while touring, and these affiliations are sought and enjoyed (Fu *et al.*, 2012).

However, there are differences among the generations *vis-à-vis* the degree to which traditional values are upheld. Beyond traditions, younger Singaporeans overtly adopt the attitude of *kiasuism* (from the term *kiasu* – a Hokkien word meaning wanting to win, or fear of losing), a tag unique to Singaporeans. This *kiasu* attitude is particularly evident in crowded situations or some competitive social contexts. For example, Nisha observes:

> On several occasions, I have observed fellow Singaporean tour group mates rushing to occupy seats in a restaurant, pushing each other to board buses or even dashing at buffet tables to fill their plates. It is very embarrassing to witness such behaviours and the disgust apparent on observers' faces; but I recognise this as the *kiasu* Singaporean attitude that we grew up with, which often unknowingly surfaces.

Cognitive reflexivity

Similar to many of our Asian counterparts, Singaporeans exhibit a rather implicit style of communication, reflecting the Confucian values of modesty and humility, and respect and harmony towards others. Unspoken rules, social protocol and etiquette govern many aspects of daily (social and business) life. Additionally, the notion of *face* is still significant for most Singaporeans. The use of direct questions, objections or 'no' is frowned upon, since this can cause loss of face for the parties involved. When communicating face to face, Singaporeans tend to limit their emotional or facial expressions, with no prolonged, direct eye contact. Often, displeasure or negative emotions are not overtly expressed, and parties may even adjust the syntax and word choices to avoid causing offence. Consequently, non-verbal signals have to be carefully observed, since a 'yes, but' will usually mean 'no'. For example, Eunice recounts:

> When socialising and travelling, I will generally avoid direct criticisms and negative comments, since it may be considered impolite and inconsiderate to my hosts. This will cause uneasiness, inconvenience and 'loss of face', which should be avoided. In the event that I need to disagree with a comment, or decline an offer (e.g. of food, an activity or a gift), I will tend to moderate my responses to avoid offence.

Mok and Defranco (2000) discuss this notion of *Mien-tzu* (face) within the context of Chinese interpersonal relationships, where face-enhancing qualities and thoughtfulness are valued. The need for respect and observance of *face* is highlighted by Nisha:

> It is important for me to feel the warmth of the host population, to be welcomed as a guest to their country and be treated with respect. While I expect friendliness from the host, they should not be informal in their behaviour towards us and encroach into our private space.

Nisha further shares:

> When I am dissatisfied with the service delivered by tourism suppliers, I tend not to overtly express my negative emotions, especially in the presence of other fellow travellers. Direct confrontations are certainly avoided. The preference is to pen down my discontent on feedback forms or via a follow-up email. Likewise, I dislike loud and unruly behaviour among fellow travellers and expressions of complaints and displeasure tend to negatively affect my experience.

Singaporeans commonly use pauses in speech and silence during communication to express a range of unspoken messages, including disagreement and displeasure; or that the person is cautiously considering what is being said. Hence, dominating a conversation by talking all the time, without pauses, may be misconstrued by Singaporeans as being impolite, boastful or insincere. Exhibiting a boastful attitude regarding one's individual achievements or possessions is not acceptable and the Western notion of 'blowing your own trumpet' is considered inappropriate. For example, Eunice reflects:

> I often find myself feeling exceedingly uncomfortable and self-conscious when offered a strong or direct compliment. While I deeply appreciate the giver's best intentions, kind words and kudos, I am often left tongue tied and awkward in my response, particularly with someone I have just met. Perhaps it is due to Buddhist teachings, Confucianism philosophy or traditional Asian customs. In such instances, I would usually express thanks and appreciation, but follow that with an effort to extenuate the accolade, so as not to come across as conceited or arrogant.

Finally, while Singaporeans may exhibit a strong focus on task accomplishment, efficiency and diligence, we also conversely strive to arrive at a consensus in decision-making, so as to not upset group harmony. Nonetheless, we have a fairly pragmatic tendency and would generally support our ideas with relevant data and hard facts. With our strong emphasis on efficiency and effectiveness, time is considered of the essence, and punctuality is deemed essential. Nisha reveals that:

> When I am part of a tour group, I value tour guides who are knowledgeable and well informed, and who provide accurate facts about the destination. However, a bossy tour guide who 'shows off' his experience is an instant put-off. They must be able to deliver what has been promised in the tour itinerary, manage the group and activities effectively and be on time. It really upsets me and spoils the whole travel experience when the guide or tour group mates are not punctual and keep the rest of us waiting.

Additionally, Nisha discloses:

> I undertake plenty of research during the pre-trip preparation, combing the internet, talking to travel agents and reading up on the destination and its culture. I tend to trust and depend on opinions and advice from my social circle in my decision-making. I get concerned and uncomfortable about leaving it to chance and being unprepared in my travel.

Physical being

Singaporeans are relatively high risk-takers by Asian standards. Although Singaporeans are generally well educated, highly adaptable, modern and considered particularly efficient individually, the Asian mentality still prevails, and most Singaporeans tend to lean towards conformism, traditional values, and respect for seniority and authority. A high degree of governmental intervention in daily life is accepted and most Singaporeans are willing to accept and abide by the strict governmental regulations and controls imposed on social behaviour (e.g. strict enforcements on drugs, smoking, littering, chewing gum and jaywalking). As customers, Singaporeans are highly astute and have high expectations, sometimes even coming across as remarkably demanding! We want quality products and services, are often knowledgeable about the specifics, and generally investigate meticulously, in order to not miss any relevant information. For example, Nisha recounts:

> Being accustomed to strict laws back home, I am afraid of jaywalking (even if everyone in the country is doing so) and tend to cross only at traffic lights…. I also consciously look for litter bins at great length and will avoid littering. Despite being in a foreign country, the inclination is to stick to the rules and regulations. So, the sight of locals peeing on the roads, vandalising, spitting and other negative social behaviours tends to be an unpleasant experience and paints a negative impression in my mind about the destination and its people.

Eunice also expresses a similar inclination when it comes to risk-taking and conformism:

> When travelling, I tend to avoid areas or places I feel unsure about or not familiar with. If I have to be in those tourism spaces, there is a tendency to avoid direct eye contact or interactions with strangers. In fact, there is usually a conscientious effort to not stand out from the crowd and/ or to draw attention to myself. While I desire and seek out new places and cultural experiences, I would prefer to soak up the ambience and appreciate the experience privately.

Pearce et al.'s (2013) similarly found that Chinese tourists exhibit a level of caution and wariness when interacting socially with local people they are not familiar with. This cautious attitude is heightened if prior warnings are given by tour guides or other travellers. While there is an inert curiosity and desire to experience new cultures and social encounters, interactions and exchanges with local hosts take time to be developed and nurtured. Fundamentally, safety is a key priority. While we seek authentic and novel travel experiences, we are also restricted to our own 'cultural bubbles' that are constrained by our gender and cultural valuation of safety and security (Asbollah et al., 2013: 687).

Spiritual being

From a young age, Singaporeans are taught to honour and commit a strong allegiance to the group (be it the family, school, neighbourhood or society). As discussed, despite our contemporary Western outlook, we still generally tend to hold a strong attachment to our ethnic, religious and cultural traditions, practices and rituals in many aspects of our day-to-day lives. For example, the Chinese respect and embrace the Confucian teachings of harmony and ordered relationships; and the Malays inculcate *Budi* (courtesy and respect – especially for elders), peace and harmony in one's family and society. In Singapore's multi-ethnic melting pot, we embrace and celebrate these diverse religious and cultural traditions regularly and comfortably. For example, Nisha reflects:

> I enjoy experiencing novelty and new experiences when I travel. However, I am not comfortable with public displays of love and friendliness, and provocative mannerisms or dress, especially when travelling with the family.

These expectations are similarly voiced by Muslim women travellers in Malaysia (Asbollah *et al.*, 2013). On an affective and spiritual level, there is also a tendency and desire to reconcile what we are seeing (gazing) and experiencing (activities) with our own inner gendered and cultural identities. As Eunice explains:

> Often, my primary motivation to travel is to seek out new experiences, cultural landscapes and affective sensations. Thus, I am usually not content to just aesthetically view a destination, its culture and environs on the surface. When touring a new tourism space, I seek meaningful experiences, poignant stories and opportunities to learn about the place, its culture and peoples. There is a desire to connect with the place cognitively, emotionally and spiritually.

Asbollah *et al.* (2013) propose the term 'spiritual gaze' to describe the experience of Muslim women travellers who view nature and the culture of the tourism destination as part of God's creation and their need to protect and conserve these resources during their travel. Pearce *et al.* (2013) similarly found that Chinese tourists tend to appreciate and envisage landscapes and places through distinct culturally tinted lenses. Moreover, similar to the social interactions in our day-to-day life, there is also a conscientious effort to respect and embrace the religion, traditions and practices of different people we encounter and interact with. As Singaporeans growing up in a multi-ethnic society, this harmony between races is fundamental to social relationships and is inculcated from a young age.

The Asian female tourist gaze: Themes

From the above discussion, we can infer that our gender and cultural orientations define our self-identities, mindset and worldviews. These tend

Table 6.3 Emic reflections of the Asian female tourist gaze

Theme	Characterisation
Emotional reflexivity	Need for relaxation, de-stressing, escaping pressures at work Cultural bubble: Familiarity with culture, and mid-centric characteristics Endorse traditional values, in-group needs, social needs, conformism Asian values, *guanxi* and *kiasuism*
Cognitive reflexivity	Need for facts, information, prior knowledge before travel Need for efficiency and effectiveness; high expectations with regard to quality Gaining new knowledge, new sense of experience Need for authenticity of culture and physical environment Emphasise regulations, control of social behaviour
Physical being	Need for physical safety, security and cleanliness General risk avoidance while at the same time seeking escape and novel experiences Unwillingness to stand out from the crowd, or draw attention to oneself
Spiritual being	Asian traditional philosophy, Confucianism and Buddhism Malay *Budi* (courtesy and respect for cultures and traditions) Concern about degradation of landscape and spiritual significance of a place

to shape the way that we see, sense and attribute meanings to tourism experiences. Table 6.3 summarises some of the key themes observed within the inherent dimensions that affect and influence the Asian female tourist gaze.

Implications and Conclusion

A tourist consumption of space, which encompasses the sights and markers at a destination, is socially and culturally constructed. However, Urry's notion of the tourist gaze has narrowly focused on the privileged white male and has been uncritically applied to Asian tourists and tourism generally. This study explored the emic voices of Asian females to gain a deeper understanding of the culturally contingent gendered gaze. A broader knowledge of the gendered complexities in tourism consumption and the influences of culture on the meaning-making process of tourists have become increasingly critical in the contemporary globalised world. This study recognises the need to have alternative insightful perspectives to knowing and understanding tourist behaviours and consumption of tourist spaces. Using an autoethnographic narrative approach, we reflected on our personal experiences, encounters and interactions with the wider world gazed through our Asian lenses. In our authoethnographic journey, we have attempted to search for the 'voice of the insider', to gain new insights and understanding of our travel experiences (Dyson, 2007: 46). The consciousness experienced during our reflexive journeys brought about a 'new worldview' rather than a 'me view' (Dyson, 2007: 45).

The conceptual model proposed provides a new perspective to re-look at the universalism of the tourist gaze. The model highlights the cultural and gender orientations of the Asian female in the way they reflect and interpret experiences within the tourism setting. This study has provided an exploratory analysis of the Asian female's mindset in the way that we are conscious of our tourism experiences. In turn, these observations will serve to provide researchers with useful points of reference *vis-à-vis* the social and cultural basis shaping manifested behaviour. In light of the growth of this promising market, there is much scope for further development in researching the Asian female tourist gaze.

References

Aitchison, C., Reeves, C. and Jordan, F. (1998) Gendered (bed) spaces: The culture and commerce of women only tourism. In C. Aitchison and F. Jordan (eds) *Gender, Space and Identity: Leisure, Culture and Commerce* (pp. 47–68). Brighton: Leisure Studies Association

Alatas, F. (2006) *Alternative Discourses in Asian Social Science: Responses to Eurocentrism.* London: Sage.

Ali, N. (2012) Researcher reflexivity in tourism studies research: Dynamical dances with emotions. In I. Ateljevic, N. Morgan and A. Pritchard (eds) *The Critical Turn in Tourism Studies: Creating an Academy of Hope* (pp. 11–26). Milton Park: Routledge.

Anderson, K. (1996) Engendering race research. In N. Duncan (ed.) *Bodyspace: Destabilizing Geographies of Gender and Sexuality* (pp. 197–211). London: Routledge.

Anderson, L. (2006) Analytic autoethnography. *Journal of Contemporary Ethnography* 35 (4), 373–395.

Asbollah, A.Z., Lade, C. and Michael, E. (2013) The tourist gaze: From the perspective of a Muslim woman. *Tourism Analysis* 18, 677–690.

Assiouras, I., Skourtis, G., Koniordos, M. and Giannopoulos, A.A. (2015) Segmenting East Asian tourists to Greece by travel motivation. *Asia Pacific Journal of Tourism Research* 20 (12), 1389–1410. doi: 10.1080/ 10941665.2014.982140.

Ateljevic, I., Harris, C., Wilson, E. and Collins, F.L. (2005) Getting 'entangled': Reflexivity and the 'critical turn' in tourism studies. *Tourism Recreation Research* 30 (2), 9–21.

Bruner, E.M. (1991) Transformation of self in tourism. *Annals of Tourism Research* 18 (2), 238–250.

Buddhabhumbhitak, K. (2010) Tourist immersion or tourist gaze: The backpacker experience. In P.M. Burns, C. Palmer and J.A. Lester (eds) *Tourism and Visual Culture: Theories and Concepts* (Vol. 1, pp. 139–149). Cambridge, MA: CABI.

Cai, L.A. and Combrink, T.E. (2000) Japanese female travelers: A unique outbound market. *Asia Pacific Journal of Tourism Research* 5 (1), 16–24.

Canton, K. and Santos, C.A. (2007) The poetics of tourist experience: An autoethnography of a family trip to Eilat. *Journal of Travel Research* 45 (4), 371–386.

Chan, B. (2007) Film-induced tourism in Asia: A case study of Korean television drama and female viewer's motivation to visit Korea. *Tourism Culture and Communications* 7 (3), 207–224.

Denzin, N.K. (1995) *The Cinematic Society: The Voyeur's Gaze*. London: Sage.
Denzin, N.K and Lincoln, Y.S. (1994) Introduction: Entering the field of qualitative research. In N.K. Denzin and Y.S. Lincoln (eds) *Handbook of Qualitative Research* (pp. 1–17). Thousand Oaks, CA: Sage.
Denzin, N.K. and Lincoln, Y.S. (2000). Introduction: The discipline and practice of qualitative research. In N.K. Denzin and Y.S. Lincoln (eds) *Handbook of Qualitative Research* (2nd edn) (pp. 1–28). Thousand Oaks, CA: Sage.
Dyson, M. (2007) My story in a profession of stories: Auto ethnography – An empowering methodology for educators. *Australian Journal of Teacher Education* 32 (1), 3.
Ellis, C. and Bochner, A. (2000) Autoethnography, personal narrative, reflexivity: Researcher as subject. In N.K. Denzin and Y.S. Lincoln (eds) *Handbook of Qualitative Research* (2nd edn) (pp. 733–768). Thousand Oaks, CA: Sage.
Ellis, C., Adams, T.E. and Bochner, A.P. (2011) Autoethnography: An overview. *Forum: Qualitative Social Research* 12 (1), 273–290.
Foucault, M. (1994) *The Birth of the Clinic: An Archaeology of Medical Perception*. New York: Vintage Books.
Fu, X., Lehto, X.Y. and Cai, L.A. (2012) Culture-based interpretation of vacation consumption. *Journal of China Tourism Research* 8 (3), 320–333.
Gladstone, D. (2006) *From Pilgrimage to Package Tour*. London: Routledge.
Hall, D., Swain, M.B. and Kinnaird, V. (2003) Tourism and gender: An evolving agenda. *Tourism Recreation Research* 28 (2), 7–11.
Heimtun, B. and Morgan, N. (2012) Proposing paradigm peace: Mixed methods in feminist tourism research. *Tourist Studies* 12 (3), 287–304.
Hofstede, G.H. (1980) *Culture's Consequences: International Differences in Work-Related Values*. Newbury Park, CA: Sage.
Hofstede, G.H. (2001) *Culture's Consequences: Comparing Values, Behaviors, Institutions and Organizations Across Nations*. Thousand Oaks, CA: Sage.
Hollinshead, K. (1999) Surveillance of the worlds of tourism: Foucault and the eye-of-power. *Tourism Management* 20 (1), 7–23.
Hughes, C. and Cohen, R.L. (2012) Feminists really do count: The complexity of feminist methodologies. In C. Hughes and R.L. Cohen (eds) *Feminism Counts: Quantitative Methods and Researching Gender* (pp. 1–9). London: Routledge.
Hughes, J.A. (1990) *The Philosophy of Social Research*. London: Longman.
Humberstone, B. and Collins, D. (1998) Ecofeminism, 'risk' and women's experiences of landscape. In C. Aitchison and F. Jordan (eds) *Gender, Space and Identity: Leisure, Culture and Commerce* (pp. 137–150). Brighton: Leisure Studies Association.
Humphreys, M. (2005) Getting personal: Reflexivity and autoethnographic vignettes. *Qualitative Inquiry* 11 (6), 840–860.
Jenkins, J. (2000) The dynamics of regional tourism organisations in New South Wales, Australia: History, structures and operations. *Current Issues in Tourism* 3 (3), 175–203.
Jucan, M.S. and Jucan, C.N. (2013) Gender trends in tourism destination. *Procedia – Social and Behavioral Sciences* 92, 437–444.
Khoo-Lattimore, C. and Prayag, G. (2015) The girlfriend getaway market: Segmenting accommodation and service preferences. *International Journal of Hospitality Management* 45, 99–108.
Kim, C. and Lee, S. (2000) Understanding the cultural differences in tourist motivation between Anglo-American and Japanese tourists. *Journal of Travel and Tourism Marketing* 9 (1–2), 153–170.
Kim, D., Lehto, X.Y. and Morrison, A.M. (2007) Gender differences in online travel information search: Implications for marketing communication on the internet. *Tourism Management* 28, 423–433.
Kim, K. and Beck, J.A. (2009) Exploring leisure trip behaviors of university women students: An investigation of push and pull motivational models. *Journal of Hospitality Marketing and Management* 18 (4), 386–405.

Kim, M., Lee, M., Lee, C. and Song, H. (2012) Does gender affect Korean tourists' overseas travel? Applying the model of goal-directed behavior. *Asia Pacific Journal of Tourism Research* 17 (5), 509–533.
Kinnaird, V. and Hall, D. (1994) *Tourism: A Gender Analysis*. Chichester: Wiley.
Kinnaird, V. and Hall, D. (1996) Understanding tourism processes: A gender-aware framework. *Tourism Management* 17 (2), 95–102.
Leung, D., Leung, R., Bai, B. and Law, R. (2011) Asian wave in travel and tourism research. *Journal of Travel and Tourism Marketing* 28 (2), 196–209.
Li, M. and Cai, L.A. (2012) The effects of personal values on travel motivation and behavioral intention. *Journal of Travel Research* 51 (4), 473–487.
Li, M., Wen, T. and Leung, A. (2011) An exploratory study of the travel motivation of Chinese female outbound tourists. *Journal of China Tourism Research* 7 (4), 411–424.
Maoz, D. (2006) The mutual gaze. *Annals of Tourism Research* 33 (1), 221–239.
McCabe, S. (2003) Gender, identity and discourse in the consumption of leisure travel: An ethnomethodological approach. *Tourism Recreation Research* 28 (2), 67–75.
Meng, F. (2010) Individualism/collectivism and group travel behavior: A cross-cultural perspective. *International Journal of Culture, Tourism and Hospitality Research* 4 (4), 340–351.
Mok, C. and Defranco, A.L. (2000) Chinese cultural values: Their implications for travel and tourism marketing. *Journal of Travel and Tourism Marketing* 8 (2), 99–114.
Noy, C. (2007) The language(s) of the tourist experience: An autoethnography of the poetic tourist. In I. Ateljevic, A. Pritchard and N. Morgan (eds) *The Critical Turn in Tourism Studies: Innovative Research Methodologies* (pp. 349–370). Milton Park: Routledge.
Pearce, P.L., Wu, M. and Osmond, A. (2013) Puzzles in understanding Chinese tourist behavior: Towards a triple-C gaze. *Tourism Recreation Research* 38 (2), 145–157.
Pernecky, T. (2007) Immersing in ontology and the research process: Constructivism the foundation for exploring the (in)credible OBE? In I. Ateljevic, A. Pritchard and N. Morgan (eds) *The Critical Turn in Tourism Studies: Innovative Research Methods* (pp. 211–226). Amsterdam: Elsevier.
Prayang, G., Cohen, S.A. and Yan, H. (2015) Potential Chinese travelers to Western Europe: Segmenting motivations and service expectations. *Current Issues in Tourism* 18 (8), 725–743.
Pritchard, A. and Morgan, N.J. (2000) Constructing tourism landscapes: Gender, sexuality and space. *Tourism Geographies: An International Journal of Tourism Space, Place and Environment* 2 (2), 115–139.
Reisinger, Y. and Turner, L.W. (2002) Cultural differences between Asian tourist markets and Australian hosts, Part 1. *Journal of Travel Research* 40 (3), 295–315.
Remoaldo, R.C., Vareiro, L., Ribeiro, C. and Santoas, J.F. (2014) Does gender affect visiting a world heritage site? *Visitor Studies* 17 (1), 89–106.
Riley, R.W. and Love, L.L. (2000) The state of qualitative tourism research. *Annals of Tourism Research* 27 (1), 164–187.
Ronai, C.R. (1992) The reflexive self through narrative: A night in the life of an erotic dancer/researcher. In C. Ellis and M.G. Flaherty (eds) *Investigating Subjectivity: Research on Lived Experience* (pp. 102–124). Newbury Park, CA: Sage.
Ryan, C. and Hall, C.M. (2001) *Sex Tourism: Marginal People and Liminalities*. London: Routledge.
Shepherd, R. (2009) Cultural preservation, tourism and' donkey travel' on China's frontier. In T. Winter, P. Teo and T.C. Chang (eds) *Asia on Tour: Exploring the Rise of Asian Tourism* (pp. 253–263). London: Routledge.
Shields, R. (1991) *Places on the Margin*. London: Routledge.
Shurmer-Smith, P. and Hannam, K. (1994) *Worlds of Desire, Realms of Power: A Cultural Geography*. London: Arnold.

Sun, L.B. and Qu, H. (2011) Is there any gender effect on the relationship between service quality and word-of-mouth? *Journal of Travel and Tourism Marketing* 28 (8), 210–224.
Swain, M.B. (1995) Gender in tourism. *Annals of Tourism Research* 22 (2), 247–266.
TMA (2015) *Country Navigator.* Transnational Management Associates Ltd. Available at https://www.countrynavigator.com (accessed May 2016).
Tribe, J. (2001) Research paradigms and the tourism curriculum. *Journal of Travel Research* 39 (4), 442–448.
Tsang, N. (2011) Dimension of Chinese culture values in relation to service provision in hospitality and tourism industry. *International Journal of Hospitality Management* 30, 670–679.
Tsang, N. and Ap, J. (2007) Tourists' perceptions of relational quality service attributes: A cross-cultural study. *Journal of Travel Research* 45 (3), 355–363.
Urry, J. (1990) *The Tourist Gaze: Leisure and Travel in Contemporary Societies*. London: Sage.
Urry, J. (1992) The tourist gaze 'revisited'. *American Behavioral Scientist* 36 (2), 172–186.
Urry, J. (2001) Globalizing the tourist gaze. Available at http://www.lancaster.ac.uk/fass/resources/sociology-online-papers/papers/urry-globalising-the-tourist-gaze.pdf (accessed May 2016).
Urry, J. and Larsen, J. (2011) *The Tourist Gaze 3.0*. New York: Sage.
Wearing, B. and Wearing, S. (1996) Refocussing the tourist experience: The 'aneur' and the 'choraster'. *Leisure Studies* 15, 229–244.
Westwood, S., Pritchard, A. and Morgan, N.J. (2000) Gender-blind marketing: Businesswomen's perceptions of airline services. *Tourism Management* 21, 353–362.
Winter, T. (2009) Asian tourism and the retreat of Anglo-Western centrism in tourism theory. *Current Issues in Tourism* 12 (1), 21–31.
Wong, I.K.A. (2013) Mainland Chinese shopping preferences and service perceptions in the Asian gaming destination of Macau. *Journal of Vacation Marketing* 19 (3), 239–251.
Yang, Y. and Wu, X. (2014) Chinese residents' demand for outbound travel: Evidence from the Chinese family panel studies. *Asia Pacific Journal of Tourism Research* 19 (10), 1111–1126.
Zhang, Y. and Hitchcock, M.J. (2014) The Chinese female tourist gaze: A netnography of young women's blogs on Macao. *Current Issues in Tourism* (published online). doi: 10.1080/13683500.2014.904845.

7 'Home' as a Mobile Cultural Diaspora: South Asian American Women and the Conceptualisation of Holidays in America

Roksana Badruddoja

Introduction

Disrupting monolithic images of South Asian Americans

South Asians are one of the fastest-growing ethnic groups in the United States, and the major influx of South Asian migration began after the Immigration and Naturalisation Act of 1965.[1] The influx of South Asian immigrants raises several scholarly questions, such as what changes occur in South Asian immigrant families when they move to the United States. However, less visible in the media and scholarship are the children of these immigrants. The offspring of the post-1965 immigrants began to come of age during the late 1980s and early 1990s, but the stories of these South Asian Americans have not adequately been told and incorporated into the larger narratives of the United States (see Maira, 2002: 2). The now adult children of these immigrants represent a critical generation, determining patterns of race, ethnicity, culture, economy and politics in the United States. Maira (2002) writes, 'Immigrant youth culture raises questions about the relationships of immigrant communities to the nation-state in which they live and the one they ostensibly left behind' (p. 21). A central question, therefore, is what kinds of cultural identities are second-generation South Asian Americans forging?[2] What are their cultural values and practices in the context of South Asian American identities?

In an attempt to answer such questions, in this chapter I examine a discursive site – celebration of holidays – in which South Asian Americans produce and consume culture. More specifically, I explore South Asian American women and how their gendered identities are negotiated in the ways in which they conceptualise 'Western' holidays like Thanksgiving in America. By doing so, I also interrogate the notion of 'home' as part of the (gendered) South Asian American imagination and landscape. Where is 'home' and what is it in the context of cultural (re-)production within the American nation-state and transnationally? I accomplish this by engaging in a year-long feminist ethnographic project with a cross-national sample of 25 'second-generation' South Asian American women

Experience/theory

Here, I view this work as a personal journey; my scholarship is personal. My academic endeavours stem from my autobiographical history (see hooks, 1990; Puar, 1994a, 1994b; Spivak, 1988). Puar's discussion about the experience/theory divide, within which this research is situated, is invaluable. She writes:

> I ... believe that the relationships between experience and theory are contingent, discontinuous, and contradictory.... Just as readers are situated in multiple discursive geopolitical positionings, I too, as an author, can situate and resituate my self and thus my text as reflective of my selves. (Puar, 1994b: 78)

Therefore, like Narayan, 'I ... wish to suggest some linkages between the complexities of who I am and what I claim to know' (Narayan, 1997: 5). I take a moment to clarify my influences.

I am a queer Muslim Bangladeshi American woman, an American offspring of a small group of pre-1965 professional Bengali immigrants (and a mother to a precocious daughter who is negotiating her 'brownness' at school). As a child and adolescent, I juggled and moved between my 'South Asian' (particularly a Muslim Bangladeshi) identity and my 'American' (read as 'honorary white') identity, which at times felt distinct to me. As a consequence of discursive colonisation, I was not 'American' enough for my classmates in elementary school and I was too 'Western' or 'corrupt' for my immigrant parents (see also Maira, 2002: 4). Similar to the Cheshire Cat in Lewis Carroll's *Alice's Adventures in Wonderland* (1865), I felt I had no bounded sense of self at times. These feelings of permeability and contamination came from the fact that I sensed there was no room to be both 'South Asian' and 'American'. In other words, this is a 'borderland' (Mohanty, 2003).

However, the project was a process of self-repair and self-recovery. In this study, the 25 women's biographies clarify my own notions of identity, guiding me towards a project of self-recovery and reconciliation with myself. The women taught me that I do not have one identity; rather, I can identify on many grounds – across race, class, gender, nationality, sexuality, etc. My identities are not constructed in isolation. They can be simultaneous and contradictory; they are not mutually exclusive, and they do not operate with equal importance in all situations. What began as feelings of isolation and the need for separation ended with a personal project of identity with multidimensional histories.

What I discover is the acceptance of, manipulation of and resistance to hegemonic cultural power – American nationalism (read as 'white' and Christian) – by an often invisible and marginalised group. In this way, I am participating in creating a canon so that later generations may be able to find guidance in telling our 'American' story.

Sociological significance

This chapter is sociologically significant because I examine perceptions and social practices – namely, celebrating holidays. Earlier studies on South Asian populations (Agarwal, 1991; Fisher, 1980; Gibson, 1988; Lessinger, 1995; Mukhi, 2000) have not paid sufficient attention to the manner in which members of those populations view themselves in comparison with broader American society. The literature on the second generation frequently underscores the process by which they are adjusting to American society (see Maira, 2002; Prashad, 2000; Purkayastha, 2005).

Two main theoretical perspectives – assimilation (Portes & Rumbaut, 2001) and pluralism (Conzen, 1991) – commonly have been the basis for examining that adjustment process. Central to the assimilation perspective is the assumption that there is a natural process by which diverse ethnic groups come to share a common culture and gain equal access to opportunities (Gordon, 1964). Alternatively, the pluralist perspective perceives American society as consisting of a harmonious collection of culturally distinct ethnic and racial groups (Zhou, 1997). I am concerned with the aspect of social life that the two perspectives tend to downplay.

While the perspectives are often characterised as different, they have two features in common that have not yet been sufficiently transcended. In both instances, the research on second-generation populations focuses on outcome: on the one hand, the result is assimilation; and on the other hand, it is a form of power sharing. Beyond their emphasis on outcome, however, both positions are fundamentally focused on the extent to which those outcomes serve to diminish social conflict within society. The 'outcome' focus can be seen as oriented towards the absorptive ability of the social system as a whole.

The ability of the social system to adapt to diverse populations is a valuable research agenda. However, it does not provide an understanding of the equally valuable research concern with the inner workings of the individuals. Grewal (1993: 53) writes, 'The debates on assimilation and nonassimilation might elide the important projects of complicity with and utilisation of difference'. This chapter indicates that second-generation individuals are engaged in the complicated process of simultaneously mediating the culture of their parents and the culture of their new society. The analysis I offer here incorporates an additional major focal point that is missing from previous literature – namely, the intersections among women, identity, colour, immigration and diasporic movement, and national belonging and the nation-state, and it questions the relationships among these variables.

This chapter is about how second-generation South Asian American women make sense of their everyday relationship with the state by interrogating their identity-making practices and discursive experiences through the portal of celebrating American holidays and what this might mean for the production of 'home' (where and what is it?). I present holidays as a discursive site because my research participants collectively offered to me – as part of an emancipatory research model (see hooks, 1990; Spivak, 1988) – the celebration of holidays in the US as a space of cathexis in which they (re-)produce and (re-)consume culture.[3] That is, I choose to explore holidays because my research participants point to this particular site in which they participate to 'make' culture. I learn from my informants that holidays serve as an important context in which to evaluate how identities are shaped, accepted and contested.

The Study

Herein, I present partial data from a year-long ethnography. In 2004, I conducted in-depth semi-structured confidential interviews with a cross-national sample of 25 second-generation South Asian American women.[4] The goal of the study was to uncover second-generation South Asian American women's perceptions of their daily social practices in the United States and the manner in which they view themselves in comparison with broader American society. I used both snowball and convenience sampling to recruit informants for the study. Each four- to six-hour interview spanned over a single day to include meal breaks. The interviews were tape-recorded and transcribed primarily in English, with Bengali words and phrases sprinkled within the conversations. The semi-structured interviews covered multiple areas of concern, including coupling, work, families, food and clothing. Although the guide was used loosely, throughout the interviews I attempted to empirically unpack how my informants saw themselves within contradictory forces of race, ethnicity, class, gender, sexuality and nationality and citizenship dimensions in the United States. I used a voice-centred relational analytical method or microanalysis as a sound methodological tool to analyse the interview transcripts (Strauss & Corbin, 1998).

Identities from a postcolonial perspective and the contradictions of multiculturalism

The Orientalist divide between South Asia and America allows for little sense of complex cultural production from multiple lineages, and this is precisely the problem (Prashad, 2000). Desi culture ('desi' derives from the Hindi word 'desh', meaning motherland; it is a diasporic identity term used by South Asians in America to refer to themselves) is treated as an ahistorical trait and as a fixed, static and boundaried state of identity. How, then, do the second generation decide or make choices about cultural identities when they do not have stories filled with different versions of the past?

The literature points to parental economic resources, class aspirations and financial anxieties as influencing the second generation's reworking of racial, ethnic and gender ideologies. Prashad (2000) discovers that many young desis do not find the 'model minority' category useful in their social lives. Children of the techno-professionals are expected to identify with white, bourgeois values, whereas the working class identify with black culture. Feeling more like people of colour than white, many desis who are second generation (and middle class) have embraced hip-hop as a medium of living and expression. Young desis in North America have fashioned their cultural politics around several icons of the black diaspora. The Punjabi bhangra (a North Indian and Pakistani style of music and dance), jungle and reggae are infused in the music of South Asian American remix artists such as DJ Rekha, filling the airwaves of New York City clubs.

Maira (2002), in her study of second-generation Indian Americans in Manhattan in the mid-1990s, attempts to discover the deeper meaning of this distinct remix Indian youth subculture and the role it plays in helping young South Asian Americans define their ethnic identity and gender relationships. She characterises the subculture by music and dance, which combines Hindi film music and bhangra with American rap, techno, jungle and reggae. Maira finds that the youths are eager participants in conservative and hegemonic politics of cultural authenticity. Most of her interview participants self-identify as Indian rather than American or even a hyphenated Indian-American (Maira, 2002: 3). And a good Indian American is a person who watches and enjoys Hindi films, demonstrates some fluency in an Indian language, socialises exclusively with other Indian Americans, and embraces a Hindu identity (the politics of ethnic authenticity) (Maira, 2002: 11). Underlying these cultural practices of the second generation is a collective nostalgia for India as a site of tradition and authentic identity (Maira, 2002: 12). However, the subculture also helps to produce a notion of what it means to be cool as a New York youth that is worked into the nostalgia for India. In other words, youth subcultures are embedded in the dialectic between presumably divergent pathways of assimilation and ethnic authenticity (Maira, 2002: 16). Indian American youngsters are trapped in a dialectic between the 'coolness' of a remix subculture and the need to be authentically ethnic. What the stories begin to hint at is that ethnic identity need not be a totalising identity and can be critically and selectively reconstructed (Maira, 2002: 4).

Prashad (2000) and Maira (2002) intelligently explore the place of collective struggle and multiracial alliances in the transformation of self and community in order to make larger comments on how Americans define themselves (see also Purkayastha, 2005). They demonstrate the inadequacy of current categories and theoretical perspectives. Both vehemently argue that the term *American-Born Confused Desis* (ABCDs) – a popular term used among South Asians in America to describe the second generation – is a pathologising term and both are critical of sociological theories of segmented assimilation that portray urban youth of colour as part of a maladaptive culture. Prashad and Maira offer interventions countering the focus on ethnic authenticity and assimilation narratives by uncovering the multiple, situational identities displayed by the second generation that are fluid, complex and hybrid.

Multiculturalism has emerged in an effort to create representation and space for those who have been marginalised in research and in practice (Asher, 2007: 55). A considerable body of literature has served to inform the academy about diverse racial, cultural and ethnic backgrounds. Postmodern and postcolonial scholars like bell hooks (1990) and Nina Asher (2007) have taken multiculturalism a step further by underscoring the intersectional nature of race, class, gender, culture, language, history and geography. Unlike cultural pluralism, an intersectional approach to multiculturalism helps us to deconstruct the fluid and contested power relations that shape identities, cultures and representations.

Yet, community, media and psychological discourses continue to pathologise second-generation South Asian Americans through the notion of ABCDs. ABCDs do not represent a clear or legitimate category in a contemporary Orientalist framework. The fundamentals of multiculturalism are important here: the one-dimensional model indicates that responses are formulated specifically so that one has to situate oneself with respect to the presumed unity of the social worlds (extreme assimilation/the melting pot) versus the alternative conception of society as a collection of discrete and divided ethnic and racial communities (extreme multiculturalism) (Hartmann & Gerteis, 2005: 220). As such, ABCDs are situated between first-generation immigrant South Asians and hegemonic Americans – an ambiguous, hybrid space. Puar (1994a) points out that dominant white gazes facilitate the discourse of relational differences between American and South Asian along cultural lines. The deployment of Orientalist categories in contemporary American society by both normative Americans (the white gaze) and South Asian Americans (the model minority myth) implies an unbridgeable cultural divide based on racial and ethnic structures. The pressure to be American or South Asian is a general strand that can be drawn from earlier studies.

In this chapter, I consciously choose to use a feminist model, which is a collaborative and non-oppressive research design, building on the researcher–researched relationship. I use an intersectional approach and anti-categorical complexity (McCall, 2001) – a cutting-edge method used by feminists and other social scientists to manage complexities produced by non-linear, intersectional research instruments – as a methodological tool to examine the lives and perceptions of second-generation South Asian American women. Feminists of colour have come to realise that there is one thing that all women have in common: multiple oppression. Some women are oppressed because they live their lives within binary categories and others are oppressed because they do not fit into dichotomous categories. But all women exist on multiple identity axes. Mohanty (1993), Anzaldúa (2001) and Sandoval (1991) agree to challenge the rigidity of identity variables and focus their attentions on the politics of difference as inflected by hierarchical arrangements. An intersectional approach is critical in understanding what it means to be a woman. An intersectional analysis allows one to recognise that women, regardless of geopolitical location, experience discrimination because they stand on multiple identity axes simultaneously or a 'matrix of domination' (Collins, 2000). An anti-categorical approach has the added benefit of managing complexities of multiple axes that are contradictory. It emphasises a range of diverse experiences from multiple identities that do not fit into rigid categories. Rather than considering identities as a given, I examine race, class, gender, culture, ethnicity and history as dynamic and intersecting. The assumption is that identities do not fit into neat little categories unless forced to do so by imposition of normative orders such as gender and race (McCall, 2001). Multiple dimensions of identity cannot be understood as autonomous and mutually exclusive components, but rather they should be understood within a dialectical framework, each identity variable feeding off each other and feeding into each other (Anzaldúa, 2001; Collins, 2000). Hence, the question is not about assimilation, nor is it about ethnic enclaves. I find that no model of identity is adequate in helping to explain the cultural choices of South Asian Americans.

What to celebrate?

While Thanksgiving and Christmas are popular holidays celebrated among my research participants – second-generation South Asian American women – the ways in which my informants celebrate the holidays are a product of flexible and fluid notions of identity along with an appreciation of one's own culture and a strategic comprehension of what it means to be American or the meaning of 'whiteness'.

Unanimously, the women voice that Thanksgiving and Christmas are their favourite holidays because there is an overwhelming feeling of 'joy and warmth' over the entire nation. Supriya says, 'I like Thanksgiving a lot. We just have a huge Thanksgiving dinner of 40 people. We just eat and chat.' Priyanka remarks, 'My most favourite holiday [i]s Christmas because it is festive for a whole month and that particular week everyone is off and people are getting together'. Rani states, 'I spend time getting gifts for everybody and I do all that'. Similarly, Ritu shares 'We would always have a tree and decorate the tree. I would buy presents for everybody in my family.' And, Laila says her favourite holidays is 'Thanksgiving, because more of my family shows up for it; everyone is always off and so everyone is around and everyone really gets into cooking and the tradition of it, and it just ends up being fun'. Meaning, as Americans, the women express that they are emotionally invested in Thanksgiving and Christmas.

Yet, collectively, my interviewees are clear about the ways in which the American nation-state (read as 'white' and Christian) constructs the meanings of holidays and dictates they ways in which they are able to (re-)produce culture. My informants state that Thanksgiving and Christmas are salient celebrations in their lives because they are government-sanctioned holidays that include the longest preset time off or vacation time in the women's professional settings (i.e. job or school). Visiting family during Eid (for my Muslim respondents), Durga Puja (for my Hindu respondents) or other 'South Asian' holidays requires formally petitioning for additional time off. For example, Supriya says,

> We do celebrate the Hindu celebrations, [but] given that we [are] in this Western culture, the Western holidays take more precedence.... Those are official holidays, and you get to travel. If you want to go home for Durga Puja, I have to take a day off.

And Ritu states, 'I know in Calcutta for Puja everybody gets new clothes. We don't do all that here. We do that for Christmas.' Rani shares,

> The holidays that we get off, Thanksgiving and Christmas.... Because that is when everyone is off, and that is when you spend time with your family.... [But Puja] is big enough ... I told [my employers] I have a religious reason, and I have to go home....

Here, my research participants resist being consumed by the white pole through the ways in which they choose to celebrate Thanksgiving and Christmas. A woman's family may have the traditional turkey and pumpkin pie for Thanksgiving accompanied by a menu of commonplace Bengali foods, like in Supriya's home: '[We] make three pumpkin pies.... We have turkey, stuffing and mashed potatoes and gravy.... The other people bring more

Indian stuff for the people that want to eat that.' Noopur says, 'so we made kind of like a chicken dish that was kind of mixed and then everything else was your stuffing and your mashed potatoes, your typical [stuff]…'. Tina states, 'Turkey … with the Indian ingredients and like just breading, like Shake and Bake … so we kind of mixed it a little bit…. [W]e've never had a full-blown, traditional turkey dinner for either Thanksgiving or Christmas.' And Mazeda says, 'We make dinner and we argue…. It's a combination of my mom's cooking and turkey and cranberry sauce.'

For Supriya, celebrating Thanksgiving is about being with her Bengali community: '[We spend Thanksgiving with] the Bengali weekenders. Our Thanksgiving is not with the non-Bengalis….' Like Supriya, Priyanka celebrates major American holidays with the Bengali community:

> We always go over to one of my mom's friend's house who hosts a Christmas party every year; it is just tradition. Practically the entire community goes to her house. We all dress up in new clothes. My mom usually wears a sari, and I wear whatever new clothes I got for Christmas, which is usually regular American clothing…. It's not the typical American Christmas dinner with turkey. It can be anything; it can be Thai, Bengali, or Chinese food, but it is not the typical meal….

Similarly, Padmini recounts a fond memory of celebrating Christmas with her Bengali in-laws:

> For Christmas – that's like a big deal somehow with my in-laws [who are staunch Hindus] – we go to [my husband's] mashi's (aunt's) house…. Nobody wears a sari or anything. Pretty much, people wear American clothes, but then we eat Indian food.

Annual commemorations of Thanksgiving and Christmas in such alternative ways – e.g. wearing a sari or having Bengali dishes on the holiday dinner table – create a commemorative narrative about events that are detached from their larger historical context (ahistorical). The dissociation of Thanksgiving and Christmas from their perceived religious and historical relevance allows my research participants flexibility in delineating the narrative boundaries to accentuate a desired moral lesson and leave out those developments that might detract from it (see Zerubavel, 1995).

I learn, then, that Thanksgiving and Christmas are important holidays in the women's lives. They feel connected to the holidays through the theme of family, community and social solidarity, which is embedded in both the contradictory discourses of US nationalism and 'South Asian' nationalism. Together, my research participants respond to the celebrations of 'American' or 'Western' holidays with insistent and imperious renegotiations of traditional images, although the structures and accompanying privileges that grant my informants such cultural renegotiations undermine the choices they make within the hegemony of the dominant space. As they challenge the 'white voyeur' in the production of culture through the holidays, they are also recasting whiteness through capitalism and class privilege.

I bring forth a central theme in the study: the persisting themes in my research participants' lives remain problematising the 'East/West' divide and American Orientalism by underscoring multiple and contradictory alliances and articulating a complex process in which the categories 'South Asian' and 'American' are mutually constitutive and exist both as opposites and in unison. This means that, in celebrating the holidays, my respondents engage in a process of 'cultural re-authenticity' (see Naber, 2006: 88). Without a doubt, then, understanding cultural (re-)production requires thinking through diverse languages, images, myths and rituals through which culture is represented and constituted. Here, the notion of 'home' becomes a salient factor that we must be concerned with while exploring culture (re-)productions within the context of race, ethnicity, gender, immigration and nationalism.

Home as mobile cultural diaspora

The configuration of 'home' is often staged as a 'situated, fixed, safe sphere, with ties to place' (Puar, 1994b: 75). 'Monolithic' or 'linear notions of home' refer to the naturalised, apparently self-evident qualities that are attached to the idea of 'home' (see Gillis, 1997). Most multicultural models assume assimilation as the benchmark and often link 'home' to a single spatial location. My informants, however, insist that 'home' must be written as ideologically constructed, not only across space but also through time. That is, home is constituted through a set of cultural practices.

Ronica voices the floating and transnational nature of home, swiftly challenging the linear teleology that often accompanies the discussion of home:

> I feel pretty strongly that if I try to create my identity here [in the United States], ignoring South Asia and my relationship to South Asia, it would totally make me feel like I was missing out, and it would make feel like I didn't have a real place in the world. In the sense of transnational, I feel real committed to going back to South Asia as often as I can and doing things there by giving back to a community that my family benefited from.... When I go to India it is very much about sharing the privilege that I have [from being an American].

Ronica comments on how post-1965 migration from South Asia (unlike migration in the 1800s) carried citizenship rights for many. The discourse of citizenship (and class privilege) has profound effects on the notion of home for immigrants, their children and subsequent generations: (American) citizenship produces transnational mobile bodies that travel freely transatlantically (from west to east to west). Puar (1994b: 87) reflects, 'I clutched on to [my passport] as proof of my right to movement, seeing the American eagle on its front as a sign of democracy, the freedom to move – the façade of citizenship'. Ronica is a 'shifting and multiply positioned' subject (with particular privileges of class and nation), resulting in a notion of diaspora that no longer uses a 'linear teleology'.

Rupa also accentuates the complexities involved in defining her sense of home within a linear teleology:

> Right after the [Bush–Gore] elections, I wrote this really depressing poem.... One of the things I wrote was, how do I call this my land when it is practically an accident that I am even here? My dad could have gotten residency in Canada or in the UK, but I ended up here. What are my ties here really? What does it mean to be Bengali or Muslim, growing up in this little shit town in [the East Coast]? Bangladesh, what does it mean that I call it 'back home'?

Rupa shows that 'home' cannot be written as 'one fixed place nor as a safe place, and movement is not only mobility but it [is] also about displacement' (Puar, 1994b: 76). Rupa suggests dissatisfaction with fixed and immobile conceptualisations of 'home'. But she also underscores that a shifting and multiply positioned notion of diaspora 'functions as a threat to certain homes while becoming the construct of home for certain Others'. It is neither a 'natural' space, nor is it nation-friendly (see Puar, 1994b: 76–77). Rupa vocalises the physical and sexual imagery that accompanies what it means to be both an American woman and a Bangladeshi woman (standards that she is far from):

> Yeah, I was born here [in the United States], but I don't have that draw; that pull, it is not the same. I currently embody everything that the majority of, at least eligible, voters hate. I am queer, Muslim, and brown. Of course I come back to my senses.... The last time I went to Bangladesh, I remember on Eid, I was decked out ... in a sari and my cousin put her wedding jewellery all over me.... We took rickshaws to another khala's [maternal aunt] house ... and on the way all the men in the street were coming up to the rickshaw and leering in my face, [asking], 'Cheley na mey?' [Boy or girl?] and they were mean.... So I am 'Othered' in that way.

Like Polanyi's (1944) 'double movement', Rupa's travelling is about privilege, but it is certainly not about freedom. Diasporic subjects like Rupa engage with struggles in 'both homes'.

Tina breaks down monolithic and linear notions of 'home' by questioning the notion of 'authentic' cultural expression. Tina describes her trepidation with joining Indian students' groups and associations at college: 'They [foreign students from India] came here to do their undergraduate or graduate work.... They thought of us as fake Indians, not authentic....' The call for authenticity puts Tina in opposition to 'fresh off the boat', or FOB, 'suggesting it is the "real" immigrant who can address the "mother country" as home and exist as its cultural authority in the West' (Puar, 1994b: 100). Rekha realised during a trip to India that she is not an 'authentic Indian'. She uses the example of her training in *kathak*, a North Indian form of classical dance, to articulate her inauthenticity. Rekha shares with me that her trip to India allowed her to discern that her interest in *kathak* had little to do with devotion to the art of dancing. Rather, dance practices and performances were about socialising and participating in her Bengali-American community in the Midwest:

> When I went to India, I saw what a real Indian was like – what it meant to be Indian in India. Here [in the United States], I am going around doing this Indian dance and I look Indian.... It [dancing] was about the social network I had myself entrenched in, which was going to parties and functions. That seemed to me almost fabricated and, most importantly, I felt like I couldn't truly represent what that [*kathak*] really was ... I am not one of those people in India. I couldn't ever truly represent that.

The women construct notions of what it means be a *real* 'South Asian' and what it means to be an 'American', and cultivate experiences of 'discovering' an 'authentic self' that are problematic (see Puar, 1994b: 84).

Tina's travels to Calcutta are captured by the legacy of the white traveller on vacation – luxury, leisure and privilege: 'People take us for granted. They think that dollars grow on trees. Every time we go back, it is assumed that we are going to treat them just because we are from the US.' Noopur observes, 'My [family in India] make comments that we have everything..... Outside of America, [life] is made out to look like we snap our fingers and five hundred dollars falls into my lap.' Ronica reflects:

> When I am in Calcutta.... It is so embarrassing to be totally singled out and treated like you are a prima donna.... What's embarrassing about that is knowing that I haven't done anything to receive that privilege or to receive that recognition [except] be born in another country.

Mohanty writes:

> Notions of home and community are located within a deeply political space, where racialisation and gender and class relations and histories

> become the prism through which [to understand], however partially, what it could mean to be South Asian in North America ... [and] the meanings attached to home and community in India. (Mohanty, 1993: 353)

My informants' histories are class-, race- and gender-specific negotiations of the transnational experience of crafting a South Asian American identity.

Bhabha provides an impressive context in which to embed my participants' experiences:

> The problematic enunciation of cultural difference becomes, in the discourse of relativism, the perspectival problem of temporal and spatial distance. The threatened 'loss' of meaningfulness in cross-cultural interpretation, which is as much a problem of the structure of the signifier as it is a question of cultural codes (the experience of other cultures), then becomes a hermeneutic project for the restoration of cultural 'essence' of authenticity. (Bhabha, 1994: 179)

The 'authentic' therefore seems to be an amorphous and constantly shifting figure, 'depending on geopolitical locations and categories, constructing the mutually exclusive either/or nature of the paradigmatic figure' (Puar, 1994b: 84). Mankekar (1994: 351) speaks wonderfully to the women's struggles in defining 'home' by foregrounding the ability of diasporic subjects to engage with struggles in 'both our "homes"'. She uses the notion of cultural bifocality to acknowledge the engagements, connections and continuities between 'discontinuous spaces'. An emphasis on continuities and connections makes room for diasporic stories that are not about loss or starting anew. In this light, the recreation of the aspects of 'home' can be seen as products of considerable effort and agency on the part of the women; the project of 'home' can be seen as reassertions of their identity – an act of choice in the face of particular constraints – rather than passive conformity with tradition.

Rethinking Multiculturalism

The space of cathexis brought to the centre of attention in this study – holidays – is a site of counter-hegemony and hegemony accompanied by both struggle and privilege. My participants show that holidays serve as an important context in which to evaluate how identities are shaped, accepted and contested. The women I interviewed reject the hegemonic conception of a unitary self. Through their practices of celebrating American holidays, my research participants show their affiliation to desiness, but they also experience whiteness or Americanness in numerous ways. Escoffier writes,

'One major limitation of identity politics and its representation in multi-culturalism is that we are all born within a web of overlapping identities and group affiliations', but we are forced to disconnect those ties to focus on only one (Escoffier, 1991: 64). Minh-ha (1989: 94) says, 'despite our desperate, eternal attempt to separate, contain, and mend, categories always leak'. The cultural practices expressed through celebrating holidays in the United States underscore the agency individuals have in asserting, enhancing, maintaining and reconstructing their cultural identities.

Here, the women involved in my fieldwork articulate their identities within a constellation of intersecting loyalties that are multiple, contradictory, shifting and overlapping. This impacts on how the women in my study have come to experience the notion of 'home'. My research participants' oral histories suggest that while citizenship privileges provide the women with invincibility, like the 'white liberal travelling subject', they have come to realise that South Asia and America are 'home and 'not-home'. The women produce a complex process of identity by affirming binary formulations such as 'South Asian' and 'American' while also redrawing the boundaries between South Asia and America (see Naber, 2006).

In this chapter we learn that individuals and groups (re-)negotiate their identities, that the flexibility of cultural identity, in both its grounding in a specific political economy and its responsiveness to situational factors, allows individuals and groups to make cultural choices.

Notes

(1) The term 'South Asia' broadly refers to Bangladesh, India, Pakistan, Nepal, Sri Lanka and Bhutan, as a single geographical area. While my intent is not to collapse individual countries and communities into one false homogenised area, I find the term 'South Asia' useful in an American context to begin to understand identity work.
(2) The term 'second-generation' refers to those who are American-born or arrived in the United States by the age of four and who have at least one foreign-born parent.
(3) In the larger study, I examine four additional discursive sites – language, religion, cooking and eating (food), and clothing – that my research participants collectively identify as spaces of cathexis in which they (re-)produce and (re-)consume culture (see Badruddoja, 2012).
(4) The interview participants were born between 1965 and 1985, primarily lived in the United States from at least the ages of 4 to 21, and have Bengali-speaking mothers who were born and lived in South Asia until at least the age of 18. Within the context of the histories of arrival of South Asians in the United States, I locate my study in three central geographical sites: central New Jersey and New York City, central Illinois and northern California.

References

Agarwal, P. (1991) *Passage from India: Post-1965 Indian Immigrants and Their Children: Conflicts, Concerns, and Solutions*. Palos Verdes: Yuvati Press.

Anzaldúa, G. (2001) La Conciencia de la Mestiza: Towards a new consciousness. In K.-K. Bhavnani (ed.) *Feminism and 'Race'* (pp. 93–107). New York: Oxford University Press.

Asher, N. (2007) Rethinking multiculturalism: Attending to Indian American high school students' stories of negotiating self-representations. In C.C. Park, A.L. Goodwin and S.J. Lee (eds) *Research on the Education of Asian and Pacific Americans* (pp. 55–79). Greenwich, CT: Information Age Publishing.

Badruddoja, R. (2012) *Eyes of the Storms: The Voices of South Asian-American Women* (2nd revised edn). San Diego, CA: Cognella Press.

Bhabha, H. (1994) *The Location of Culture*. London: Routledge.

Collins, P.H. (2000) It's all in the family: Intersections of gender, race, and nation. In U. Narayna and S. Harding (eds) *Decentering the Center* (pp. 156–176). Bloomington, IN: Indiana University Press.

Conzen, K.N. (1991) Mainstreams and side channels: The localization of immigrant cultures. *Journal of American Ethnic History* 10, 5–20.

Escoffier, J. (1991) The limits of multiculturalism. *Socialist Review* 21 (3/4), 61–73.

Fisher, M.P. (1980) *The Indians of New York City: A Study of Immigrants from India*. New Delhi: Heritage.

Gibson, M.A. (1988) *Accommodation Without Assimilation: Sikh Immigrants in an American High School*. Ithaca, NY: Cornell University Press.

Gillis, J.R. (1997) *A World of Their Own Making: Myth, Ritual, the Quest for Family Values*. Cambridge, MA: Harvard University Press.

Gordon, M.M. (1964) *Assimilation in American Life: The Role of Race, Religion, and National Origins*. New York: Oxford University Press.

Grewal, I. (1993) Reading and writing the South Asian diaspora: Feminism and nationalism in North America. In Women of South Asian Descent Collective (eds) *Our Feet Walk the Sky: Women of the South Asian Diaspora* (pp. 226–236). San Francisco, CA: Aunt Lute Books.

Hartmann, D. and Gerteis, J. (2005) Dealing with diversity: Mapping multiculturalism in sociological terms. *Sociological Review* 23 (2), 218–240.

hooks, b. (1990) *Yearning: Race, Gender and Cultural Politics*. Boston, MA: South End Press.

Lessinger, J. (1995) *From the Ganges to the Hudson: Indian Immigrants in New York City*. Boston: Allyn and Bacon.

Maira, S. (2002) *Desis in the House: Indian American Youth Culture in New York City*. Philadelphia, PA: Temple University Press.

Mankekar, P. (1994) Reflections on diasporic identities: A prolegomenon to an analysis of political bifocality. *Diaspora: A Journal of Transnational Studies* 3 (3), 349–371.

McCall, L. (2001) *Complex Inequality: Gender, Class, and Race in the New Economy*. New York: Routledge.

Minh-ha, T. (1989) *Women Native Other*. Bloomington, IN: Indiana University Press.

Mohanty, C.T. (1993) Defining genealogies: Feminist reflections of being South Asian in North America. In Women of South Asian Descent Collective (eds) *Our Feet Walk the Sky: Women of the South Asian Diaspora* (pp. 351–358). San Francisco, CA: Aunt Lute Books.

Mohanty, C.T. (2003) *Feminism Without Borders: Decolonizing Theory, Practicing Solidarity*. Durham, NC: Duke University Press.

Mukhi, S.M. (2000) *Doing the Desi Thing: Performing Indiannes in New York City*. New York: Garland.

Naber, N. (2006) Arab American femininities: Beyond Arab virgin/American(ized) whore. *Feminist Studies* 32 (1), 87–111.

Narayan, U. (1997) *Dislocating Cultures: Identities, Traditions, and Third World Feminism*. New York: Routledge.

Polanyi, K. (1944) *The Great Transformation*. Boston, MA: Beacon.

Portes, A. and Rumbaut, R.G. (2001) *Legacies: The Story of the Immigrant Second Generation*. Los Angeles, CA: University of California Press.

Prashad, V. (2000) *The Karma of Brown Folk*. Minneapolis, MN: University of Minnesota Press.

Puar, J. (1994a) Resituating discourses of 'whiteness' and 'Asianness' in northern England. *Socialist Review* 24 (1–2), 21–53.

Puar, J. (1994b) Writing my way 'home': Traveling South Asian bodies and diasporic journeys. *Socialist Review* 24 (4), 75–108.

Purkayastha, B. (2005) *Negotiating Ethnicity: Second-Generation South Asian-Americans Traverse a Transnational World*. New Brunswick, NJ: Rutgers University Press.

Sandoval, C. (1991) U.S. third world feminism: The theory and method of oppositional consciousness in the postmodern world. *Genders* 10, 1–24.

Spivak, G.C. (1988) Can the subaltern speak? In C. Nelson and L. Grossberg (eds) *Marxism and the Interpretation of Culture*. Chicago, IL: University of Illinois Press.

Strauss, A. and Corbin, J. (1998) *Basics of Qualitative Research Techniques and Procedures for Developing Grounded Theory*. Thousand Oaks, CA: Sage.

Zerubavel, Y. (1995) *Recovered Roots: Collective Memory and the Making of Israeli National Tradition*. Chicago, IL: University of Chicago Press.

Zhou, M. (1997) Growing up American: The challenge confronting immigrant children and children of immigrants. *Annual Review of Sociology* 23, 63–95.

8 My Journeys in Second Life: An Autonetnography

Rokhshad Tavakoli

Introduction

I am an Iranian woman who was born in 1979 in Iran, right after the Islamic Revolution. When I was two, the conventional war between Iraq and Iran began and continued for eight years. These two events created a very fanatic Islamic environment in the country, in which women were strictly controlled by religious patrons. Dress in public was regulated by governmental authorities. These regulations were more severe for women than men; although they are less restrictive than 30 years ago, they still exist. Consequently, Iranians have been performing their 'social selves' in the public sphere in a different way than in private. As a result, some people's patterns of public behaviour, particularly women's, are quite different when abroad, due to higher perceived levels of freedom.

Besides governmental control of behaviour in public, a patriarchal society has let men have control over the female members of the family. As such, solo travelling for single girls is not allowed until they turn 18, and unless permitted by their guardians. Also, married woman need official permission to travel apart from their husbands. Single women are by law free to travel abroad, but their guardians have the authority to stop them. Iranian women face several limitations on travel inside Iran and, due to the international political situation, many countries refuse to grant Iranians visas (Tavakoli & Mura, 2016).

I had the dream of travelling around the world, like most of my young peers, but because of all these limitations, travelling alone was impossible. Consequently, when I began my undergraduate studies in software engineering I started contemplating the idea of free travel via the internet. Since my idea of tourism was more related to understanding other cultures rather than participating in leisure activities, obtaining information about other people through the internet or software simulation was the best possible use of virtual travel. However, many websites, and particularly social networks, have been filtered by the government in Iran.

When I moved to Malaysia to undertake my postgraduate studies, it was interesting for me to observe our (Iranian women's) different performances when we are free from religious patrons. More specifically, as I was intrigued by the emerging field of virtual tourism. I started to conduct research on Iranian Muslim women's behaviour during their virtual travels (Tavakoli & Mura, 2015). These 'netnographic' studies began revealing many aspects of Iranian women's online behaviour. The narratives I have collected through all these ethnographic 'journeys' unveil hidden relationships of power, which vary according to who is telling the story and who is writing it.

Who is telling what to whom?

As an ethnographer I have used myself as an instrument to explore others' worlds, give voices to other people's narratives through my views and analysis and bridge different realities. My reflexive approach to research creates a strong connection between me, a researcher, and the participants. It is a bond that undoubtedly provides additional meanings to the research I have been conducting. However, while a reflective approach may not always lead to detailed reports of the researcher's involvement in the field, autoethnography enables the researcher to have more space to express her or his 'selves'.

Scholars conducting ethnography and auto-ethnography provide very insightful information about the actual life of a community. However, they often neglect the idea that nowadays most of us have a parallel life in the virtual worlds of the internet. The importance of studying people in the virtual realm lies on the fact that people's patterns of behaviour on the internet are different from those in actual life. Therefore, netnography and autonetnography are important methodologies to unveil these relatively unknown patterns of online behaviour. These are forms of ethnography whose context of study is virtual environments, such as chat rooms or social media networks. These studies try to provide a better understanding of the various community members' behaviours in the virtual settings. Few scholars have published netnographic accounts in tourism studies, according to Mkono and Markwell (2014), and none has focused on autonetnography.

In this chapter, 3D virtual worlds are considered virtual destinations for virtual tourists. I highlight my own experiences through an autonetnography in a virtual 3D world named Second Life. Highlighting my own travel experiences in virtual destinations enables me to share detailed representations of my virtual journeys, which I would not be able to portray in detail in a netnographic study. Through this autonetnography, I explore different aspects of my virtual genders, the role of my nationality, ethnicity, religion and age, and how all these influence my behaviours and experiences as a virtual tourist.

The chapter is divided into four main parts. First, I focus on the notion of ethnography. Second, I discuss the tenets of autoethography. Third, I introduce and critically analyse the concept of nethnography. I then present the notion of autonetnography and discuss it in light of my own virtual journeys. First, though, within this introduction it will be useful to comment on gender identity in virtual worlds and to set out the methodological approach.

Virtual gender identity

Spears and Lea (1994: 428) believe that computer-mediated communication 'can serve to reduce the social barriers to communication and thus the impact of status differentials, resulting in greater equality of participation'. There is no doubt that cyberspace greatly reduces the barriers we face in the many forms of inequality. Spears and Lea's (1994) assumption applied particularly well to the early years of cyberspace, when people used to communicate in text-based environments, where 'gating features' were absent (Ben-Ze'ev, 2004: 37). These gating features, such as sex, age, social class, disability and attractiveness, provide personal information about the message sender's identity in online communications, which could be hidden behind fake IDs. This may lead some researchers to assume that virtual environments are gender-neutral contexts. Despite this, the results of linguistic studies unveil that gender inequalities persist even in text-based forms of communication (Herring, 2000). As such, the employment of technology may not result in enhanced forms of social equality and may not challenge the impact of socio-cultural and political factors on its usage and adoption (Eisenchlas, 2012).

Some researchers have found that stereotypical aspects of gender are reinforced, rather than challenged, in online communications (Tavakoli & Mura, 2015). For instance, studies of online environments show that women are still underrepresented on virtual bulletin boards and web pages (Herring, 2004), while in mixed-sex virtual public domains men are still the dominant gender. Dunn and Guadagno (2012) claim that in online environments women are shopping and men are constructing. Likewise, Herring (2000) believes that gender disparities persist in virtual environments. Huffaker and Calvert (2005) also point out that most users have a tendency not to give their real names in online unprofessional contexts. Also, while research by Palomares and Lee (2010) reveals that the silence of gender identity increases in gender-related interactions, Tavakoli and Mura (2015) found that users behave in a gender-consistent manner on their online journeys.

Methodological approach

The notion of autonetnography may seem very new, but it is rooted in an established methodological approach, namely ethnography. Autonetnography is more than sharing personal online experiences, as it requires a very strong connection between the author's actual life and his or her virtual community lifestyle. An ethnographic study may represent a general overview of a community's culture through individuals' experiences. However, an autoethnography is important as it is a 'self-observation' and 'reflexive investigation' in the researcher's life context (Maréchal, 2010: 43). Moreover, autoethnographers may not be able to share every detail of their experiences, for both political and social reasons. Netnography and autonetnography share common points. However, respondents and researchers may hide a larger part of their experiences while online, as they have the option of anonymity in virtual environments. Moreover, all these forms of ethnography are strongly interrelated, as actual and virtual experiences can influence each other. In this chapter, I provide an illustration of Iranian Muslim women's life in Iran (ethnography) and my own experience in that context (autoethnography). Then I explain how the internet changed my life and how people behave in a virtual environment (netnography). Finally, I write about my own virtual experiences in virtual worlds.

Ethnography

The etymology of the word 'ethnography' stems from the Greek words *ethnos*, meaning 'people or tribes', and *graphia*, meaning 'writing'. Interestingly, the word *ethnos* was not originally used to refer to all people but was employed to indicate 'non-Greek people'. This leads us to question the validity of early so-called ethnographical accounts (Scott-Jones & Watt, 2010), as they were probably based on biased accounts of other peoples and tribes. Ethnography in the old sense goes back to classical times, as many descriptive explanations have been found from civilised societies many centuries ago, which, although they are considered valuable attempts, are highly ideological, playing the role of justifiers for colonisation and imperialistic tendencies. The portrayal of northern European tribes by Romans as cannibalistic barbarians (Arens, 1979) is an example of this phenomenon and reiterates the root of ethnography as a description of 'others', or 'not us'. Therefore, it should be noted that many of these accounts, which are extravagant descriptions of 'others' and highly fictitious, can by no means be unbiased and neutral.

Ethnography used to be viewed as a research method, a tool for data collection, rather than a methodological approach in a theoretical framework. The latter meaning appeared in the late 19th century. Evolutionism, positivism and imperialism led to the acknowledgement of ethnography as a research method. Positivism, as the main theoretical position of the social sciences, emerged in the early 19th century and started to exploit scientific foundations to study modern societies, with an emphasis on empiricism (focusing on the role of experience and evidence and especially sensory experience) in order to derive laws or theories, just like a physicist. Moreover, the dominant theoretical realm within which social scientists tended to work was evolutionism (influenced highly by Darwin), which showed the evolution of cultures as more or less like the evolution of animals, so that one could study 'primitive' cultures in order to understand modern culture, just as the evolution of primitive organisms helps us to understand complex organisms. But in the 19th century, Europeans extended their boundaries and colonised parts of Africa and Asia. Being confronted with new cultures led them to 'scientific curiosity' and 'ideological agendas', and to justify their colonial ambitions they produced stereotypes and clichés of the colonised societies. Stereotypes like 'uncivilised', 'barbaric' and 'primitive' are very common among the colonisers' accounts, mostly written by individuals with no training in social sciences, like military officers, physicians and civil servants. Hence, what have been left are accounts with a lack of contextualisation which were fabricated to match contemporary models rather than developing new comprehension of social models. But by the end of the 19th century, social scientists had noticed the importance of fieldwork and conducted their research 'out there'.

Bronisław Malinowski (1884–1942) took up this idea and immersed himself in New Guinea's customs and culture (Kuper, 1996). His notion of ethnography was 'to grasp the native's point of view, his relation to life, to realise his vision of his world' (Malinowski, 1922: 25). By engaging himself in a daily routine in New Guinea and learning their language, culture, history and customs, Malinowski studied the culture at 'first hand' and at the same time drew many cross-cultural comparisons in his observations. As the Malinowskian revolution shifted its attention to fieldwork and the idea of linking data to social theory, some critics believe that Malinowski's idea could be misinterpreted, since he immersed himself solely in 'non-Western cultures'. While French and British sociologists chose positivism as their methodology and studied Western cultures with quantitative, empirical methods, German scholars opted for interpretivist approaches. Some American schools (notably the Chicago School) followed the German model. The first wave of feminism and all its related socio-political movements of the 1960s created the conditions for these new notions to enter the social science arena and, eventually, after the second wave of feminism, scholars were able to challenge the male-dominated ethnographic world. 'Poststructuralism' started to be employed to scrutinise the notion of power and understand knowledge structures (Foucault, 1972; Lévi-Strauss, 1968; Lyotard, 1984).

Post-structuralism resulted in 'more equal' ways of representing the 'Other' as it shifted the focus to non-Western cultures in the colonial and postcolonial periods. Also, it proposed a new notion of the ethnographer, namely a researcher who desires to become completely involved in the subject matter of study. Two important approaches, emic and etic, were brought to the fore as critics attempted to define 'best practices' for ethnographers (Kottak, 1996).

By taking emic approaches, the researcher can have an 'insider perspective'. However, it was also noted that this approach might limit the ethnographer's understanding of the 'Other'. In this regard, etic approaches can be more beneficial, as they cover the subject from an 'outsider perspective'. Modern critics simply labelled the two approaches as markers along the continuum of styles or different level of analysis (Fetterman, 2010). Another important aspect of ethnography concerns the use of reflexivity during the research process. In this regard, the researcher is perceived as the key factor in providing meaningful research outcomes. As Gilgun (2010) suggests, the researcher should reflect on three important aspects while conducting research, namely the topic of investigation, the participants and the audience. However, many authors neglected the importance of the researchers' reflection upon their experiences. Autoethnography could be a way for providing researchers' reflection.

Autoethnography

The term 'autoethnography' started to be employed in the 1970s to identify an 'insider ethnography' (Hayano, 1979: 100). Critics believe that while ethnography gives voice to the participants' views and mixes them with the researcher's own perspectives, autoethnography focuses on the researcher's voice. Ellingson and Ellis (2008) support this idea by claiming that 'whether we call a work, an autoethnography or ethnography depends as much on the claims made by authors as anything else' (p. 449). They also refer to autoethnography from two perspectives, analytic and evocative. The 'analytic autoethnographers focus on developing theoretical explanations of broader social phenomena, whereas evocative autoethnographers focus on narrative presentations that open up conversations and evoke emotional responses' (p. 445).

Richardson (2000) presents some validity techniques regarding personal narrative papers using evaluative and constructive analysis. He suggests that some important factors, including substantive contribution of the work, the aesthetic of the written work, being reflexive, the 'impactfullness' of the work, expression of reality and challenging any movement or questions, must be taken into consideration. Bochner (2000) emphasises crucial elements which are similar to those proposed by Richardson. While Bochner's 'concrete details' match Richardson's 'expression of lived experience', his 'structurally complex narratives' are similar to Richardson's 'aesthetic merit'. While Bochner's 'digging under the superficial to get to vulnerability and honesty' evokes Richardson's reflexivity, his 'standard of ethical self-consciousness' mirrors Richardson's substantive contribution. Bochner's 'moving story' also seems to represent Richardson's impact (Ellis, 2004: 253).

Netnography

According to Kozinets (2002), in a netnographic approach the researcher must identify the target and community and then gather data using one or more communities according to predetermined criteria. Researchers should also enter one or more communities with or without introducing themselves and gather data on all the participants involved while observing their interactions and communication culture. It seems that there have been a few changes in online communities through a process of fragmentation, proliferation and maturation which should be analysed very carefully and Kozinets (2006) also warns about bounded forum-type online communities that are losing their privileged status within online community research. Kozinets (2010) challenges the bounded community as he believes that these communities are becoming delocalised due to their increasing spillover to services such as YouTube, Facebook and blogs.

The growing number of netnographic studies in tourism shows that tourism scholars have begun to use the internet for their fieldwork (Mkono, 2013). Netnography enables tourism researchers to have access to rich data through online conversations or shared video materials contributed by individuals and businesses. This type of netnography is widely used in tourism marketing and the study of consumer behaviour (Munar *et al.*, 2013). Moreover, the growing amount of 'user-generated content' (UGC) on the web, whereby tourists are able to look for information and share their travel experiences, provide a great opportunity for tourism scholars to analyse tourist behaviour (Mkono & Markwell, 2014). Most tourism netnographic studies have been conducted with UGC, particularly product reviews of, for instance, destinations, as Mkono and Markwell (2014) found out. However, many studies tend to refer to web 2.0 and very few researchers (see Tavakoli & Mura, 2015) have used web 3.0, in which virtual travels happen in virtual worlds, for fieldwork.

Autonetnography

The relevance of autonetnography arises in the context of researchers' subjective and intersubjective framing of the online Self, which in turn affects how they comport themselves within virtual and other worlds, in and outside of their research activities and how they will be regarded by other members of online groups and communities. (Mkono et al., 2015: 167)

Autonetnography, like autoethnography, is based on the epistemological stand of the researchers and the way they critically include themselves in the analysis. An autonetnography cannot be detached from a netnography, as the researchers analyse themselves based on the online community's norms and values. In some cases netnographers do not report their refelexive thoughts, as they feel that their reflexion upon the research process may not be relevant to the research. However, no analysis of research products should transcend the researchers' reflexion.

Kozinets and Kedzior (2009) define autonetnography as the researcher's own experience through online participation and observation, reflexion on the field, self-image and the researcher's own narrative. An autonetnography allows the researcher the opportunity for 'experimentation', 'introspection' and 'self-observation' through ethnographic processes (Mkono et al., 2015: 167), and to reveal the hidden part of her or his virtual reality experiences, the part that many people may not want to share.

Autonetnography should not be dislocated from the researcher's autoethnography, as anyone's virtual behaviour is influenced by his or her actual experiences. In this chapter I try to provide a deep insight into my own experience in online virtual worlds and specifically in Second Life. To give meaning to my autonetnography, I provide a very brief autoethnography, which is mixed with my general autonetnography. My life journey narrative, which gives an overview of the socio-political context of my experience in Iran, may help readers to have a better understanding of my virtual behaviour. Below, I demonstrate the connection between ethnography and autonetnography, by providing a detailed narrative of the evolution of the actual and virtual contexts of my life. Following this, I explain my personal virtual world and how I shaped my virtual selves through my avatar. Then, I analyse my virtual gendered identities during this journey.

My life journey

The 1980s

I was born in 1979, right after the Islamic Revolution in Iran. When I was two, the longest conventional war started between Iran and Iraq. My childhood was influenced by this difficult scenario. During these eight years of war and sanctions, besides the limitation of food and fossil fuels, the possibility of having colourful toys and dolls did not exist, as toys were part of the imposed sanctions and considered luxury items. Boys and girls were segregated at school. At the girls' schools I went to, wearing the hijab was compulsory; indeed, under the Islamic law, all girls as soon as they reached the age of nine years had to do so. Scarfs, long shirts, trousers and shoes (all black, brown or deep blue) were the school uniform for girls. We were not even allowed to wear white socks. As these rules were also applied in public spaces, young people were not allowed to wear colourful clothes outside the domestic realm. Men were not allowed to wear t-shirts in public. Following fashion was against Islamic rules but even though access to fashion magazines was limited, we were able to obtain smuggled copies.

Meanwhile, there was little connection with the outside world and technology (e.g. the internet) was not accessible to the wider public. Newspapers and television channels were controlled by the government. Only selected movies were shown on TV and most of them were dramas about the war, with a high level of censorship. These rules were applied to children's programmes as well. Listening to any kind of Western or Iranian music with non-approved lyrics was forbidden, as it was labelled 'non-halal'. Only the radio linked us to other worlds. It was common for many young people to record banned songs (Western and Iranian) from radio channels. Overall, I could say, happiness was controlled by the government and Islamic leaders. These years were the starting point for shaping many people's multiple identities, including their gendered ones. Many Iranians embraced different gendered and non-gendered identities according to the context in which they were performing (e.g. private and public spheres).

The 1990s

After the war, in the 1990s, when I was a teenager and not exposed to any culture outside Iran, I adopted Islamic culture fanatically. I was following every Islamic rule with the intent of not breaching any of them. There was a very strong relationship between being a 'good' Iranian woman and wearing the veil. Imposing the veil was a way to create uniformity; as such, we did not know the importance of individual identity. As a result, we were objectified in that context and we lost our subjectivity. In these years we learnt how to be obedient women (daughter, wife and mother) and 'proper' Muslim women. We were taught how to avoid contact with non-mahrams. We were advised not to talk to them unless it was necessary. Applying makeup and wearing perfume were considered sinful. Wearing makeup in public was not allowed, and this was enforced by religious patrols.

Premarital sexual behaviours were not tolerated by society and families. Therefore, the chance of understanding our sexual orientation was jeopardised by the social context. In Islam only one sexual orientation officially exists and that is 'straight'. Homosexuality and bisexuality are a criminal offence and can lead to sentences like lashes or the death penalty.

At the time, video games and cassettes were smuggled into Iran and represented one of the few ways for us to be connected with the outside world.

Imported videos were considered a 'Western cultural attack', as the content of the videos was not approved by the Islamic leaders. The videos could be movies, musical shows or porn movies. Smuggling this material was a serious criminal offence and the offender could be sentenced to lashes or prison based on 'how bad' the content of the videos was. However, it was a public secret; the majority of people had video players and cassettes. I could remember the way people moved these video players and cassettes around; they were wrapped in blankets to hide them from the Islamic patrols, which often searched cars at road blocks at night. Religious authorities were not the only 'filter'; parents and relatives were also involved in this process of controlling the content of the videos.

In this decade video games became popular among youngsters. Males were the majority of the game players, as the games were largely designed for them. Video games, like other media, received criticism from the religious authorities, as they often included sexual themes, depictions of violence and promotion of alcohol and drugs. However, this would not stop young generations 'consuming' them (and even becoming addicted to them). The first generation of video gamers were single users, as the players were able to interact only with computers, but soon network games were introduced. Network games allowed groups of people to play together in game-net shops. These game-net shops were unisex (only for men).

In the late 1990s, personal computers became affordable and available to the public. At the same time, internet demand increased. As a consequence, new rules were implemented to control the content of CDs and digital data and after a while many internet web pages were filtered by the government. At this time I had started studying computer engineering at a local university, where we were not allowed even to talk to our male colleagues. We had unisex classes for social science courses and mixed classes for technical ones. Even during technical classes, we had to sit in different rows. However, the internet opened for us new gates to the outside world. Besides the useful information that we could exchange with others, the internet tools like messaging and social networks changed our social life drastically. Online dating sites mushroomed and friendship requests were sent to us from other countries. Virtual relationships were quite strange for me and many of my friends, who never had boyfriends. These requests were not limited to friendships (requests somehow perceived as normal by us), but also included sexually explicit material. In fact, I received hundreds of sex-related messages and videos every week. That made me emotional about my identity as I felt 'objectified' by this male attitude.

The 2000s

Hijab restrictions became much less severe in the early 2000s. Women were allowed to wear colourful dresses in public, although religious patrols were still heavily present on the streets. The political situation became more open for feminist activists and a few movements started. However, after 2005 women's rights declined again due to political changes in Iran. Again, hijab restrictions increased and many young people were arrested for not complying with the Islamic dress codes. This situation led many women to travel outside the country, although achieving this freedom of movement was not easy for many of us.

Television, satellites and the internet had a revolutionary effect on the socio-cultural context in Iran. After the 1979 Islamic Revolution, the Islamic Republic of Iran Broadcasting (IRIB) was the only broadcaster that provided legal channels in Iran and the content of the programmes was strictly controlled and censored by the authorities. During these years, Persian-language entertainment satellite channels started to provide programmes, which were broadcast illegally into the country. Many people began having satellite dishes at home, even if these were officially banned. Despite the attempt to stop this practice, satellite channels had millions of viewers. These channels provided news that was elsewhere censored by the government and they were available online as well. Although the internet bandwidth was kept narrow and many filters were applied to social media websites, many people managed to use anti-filtering systems. Social media usage drastically increased and it became a platform for social and political movements.

The 2010s

You can rarely find an Iranian occupying a governmental role using her or his actual name in social networks, especially if these online platforms discuss topics not allowed by Islamic rules. The risk of being accused of anti-Islamic behaviour would be too high. Therefore, many Iranian netizens usually have two online accounts, one for their professional life and one for the personal sphere. The personal account sometimes is used as a mask to experience and express disallowed behaviours anonymously. For instance, many people approach each other with fake IDs for sexting or even erotic video chats. I am a target, as I receive many friend requests per day specifically for this reason. I have to ignore them and most of the time block that ID. It gives me a horrible feeling, thinking about how these guys approach me for some kind of virtual relationship. However, healthy virtual relationships are also common, as many young Iranian netizens find the social networks a platform for having free relationships. In many cases virtual relationships end with marriage, but in some other cases they are a form of sexual harassment.

This space of freedom was once again limited in early 2011 by the Iranian cyber police (the FATA). Initially this was an attempt to control political movements, but it was soon used to control anti-Islamic behaviours. Many people have been arrested for blogging against politicians or for displaying antisocial behaviour. Even Iranians who live outside Iran are not exempt:

if the FATA detects their activities they may be arrested once they return to Iran.

In 2010 I moved to Malaysia, a very different Muslim country. There were no hijab restrictions for non-Malaysian Muslims and social media had less filters. I had freedom of speech (although still partially limited). This move was a great opportunity for me, as I started using social networks not only for communication but also for learning, an opportunity that has increased my knowledge and creativity. I am using this opportunity to conduct my research in virtual environments, as these realities are not filtered in Malaysia. I often travel in Second Life, one of the most famous 3D social networks, which is also the place where I conduct my fieldwork for my netnographic research (Tavakoli & Mura, 2015).

My autonetnography

My autonetnography is shaped by four different perspectives: first, the evolution of my life experiences and the way they contributed to form the different 'my selves'; second, outsiders' perception of 'my selves', which influence my identity; third, my perception of my virtual identities; and finally, others' perception of my virtual identities.

My enthusiasm for writing an autonetnography derives from the perception of having a different story from others' narratives, although my narratives are shaped by, and at times merge with, others' experiences. My personal world is unique and complex but it could tell stories about other worlds, which may have similar socio-cultural foundations (e.g. being Muslim, being Iranian, being a woman). By telling my story I let others participate in my imaginary worlds. I also give voice to others' stories through my own narratives. My virtual travel behaviour in Second Life is influenced by the norms, values and religion of my place of origin but at the same time it is shaped by the virtual environment's norms and values, as well as others' behaviour. Time and space also play a very important role in the way I experience virtuality. In this part of the chapter I will discuss my personal experiences in Second Life through my virtual gender identity lens.

My personal virtual world

Surfing virtual worlds was a dream of mine in the 1990s, when I was in my 20s, because it gave me the ability to travel and communicate in a barrier-free world. In my life I have experienced plenty of limitations to travel. Before any trip, besides constraints related to my nationality, age and financial resources, I had to seek my father's permission. I have always been interested in visiting historical sites and museums as I am curious about different cultures. There has always been a question at the back of my mind: when virtual travel becomes more accessible for many in contemporary society, why should we engage in old-fashioned corporeal patterns of mobility? Although there were very few sites and commercial CDs designed to promote destinations in the 1990s, they were not providing interactive environments and were rather boring.

Moreover, as a Muslim girl a lot of limitations hampered my plans to travel alone. My family was worried about my safety and security. I was living in a society that criticised girls who travelled alone, and I would be in trouble if my government realised that I was not acting as a 'proper' Muslim girl outside the national borders. Therefore, travelling virtually was a promising way to escape from all these different types of limitations. I started to surf the internet to escape from these problems and limitations. I created private IDs to enter chat rooms anonymously (in order to protect my image as a 'good' girl). Although I was happy to have the opportunity to avoid the above-mentioned problems, I still felt guilty that I had to use nicknames or avatar pictures during my virtual interactions.

I did not wear a hijab on my virtual journeys, although my beliefs, which had been transmitted to me by my social context since I was a child, still affected my patterns of behaviour in virtual environments. I tried to be 'someone else' and to wear less conservative clothes, but I could not overcome the strict rules imposed on me by the society in which I grew up.

My virtual selves

My avatar

The image of my 'selves' I create while travelling virtually is a combination of how I see myself in the mirror and how others perceive my persona. In virtual environments, the choice of my identity is complex, as I have a chance to be myself or to create an avatar that many would not perceive as 'me'. In Second Life, I have the possibility to portray my body in whatever way I like. The new virtual body, my avatar, does not necessarily need to represent my actual body. So how should I craft my avatar? Should my avatar be female or male? Blue eyes or my own eye colour? Should I craft it with a fit body or with extra pounds, like my own body? What type of hairstyle should I choose, and what colour? What should I wear? And many other questions come to my mind. I never thought that crafting my avatar with a new identity would have involved so many emotions.

In Table 8.1 I compare my actual body with my virtual embodiment. As I reflect upon the choice of my virtual body, I realise that my avatar is quite similar to my actual body and dress code. But why do I act like that, as I have a chance to change everything? I believe that my choice is based on the fact that I would feel guilty if my avatar did not resemble my actual body: I would feel like I am lying to others! I am scared of being judged by others

Table 8.1 A comparison of my actual body with my virtual embodiment

My actual body	My avatar
A tall girl with extra pounds, curly dark-brown hair, white skin and brown eyes, wearing glasses. I wear a shirt and trousers most of the time. I have to wear a headscarf when I am in public spaces in Iran	A tall girl with extra pounds, short, straight light-brown hair, white skin and brown eyes without glasses. My avatar also wears a shirt and trousers. I do not wear a hijab here

if they discover my actual physical identity. In other words, even if Second Life gives me the possibility to choose freely, I do not want to break the trust that has been given to my avatar.

My virtual gender identity

Second Life provides different identities through suggested avatars, such as animals, vehicles, vampires and robots, while some of them represent a specific gender. For example, there are pink female robots with makeup and male vampires with masculine bodies. Even some of the vehicles are designed for men or women. Why is gender still important even in virtual environments? Why should I even choose my gender? Why are virtual environments not gender-free spaces? Does gender equality have any meaning there?

When I was a teenager many times I wished I could be a boy, a sentiment shared by many of my female friends. We were overwhelmed by all the restrictions that women had in Iran at that time. However, when I had the chance to change my gender in Second Life after 20 years, I still chose to be a woman. My gender identity even influences my avatar's appearance and behaviour. Usually I do not choose stylish feminine dresses and sophisticated hairstyles. Also, I rarely behave like other female avatars. I am not like most of the users, who are very sensitive and picky about the choice of their avatar, as it is not important for me to be similar to my avatar. My experience contradicts the findings of Schroeder's (2002) research, which found that people like to have control over their avatar design. He also found that people tend to design avatars very carefully, to be as realistic as they can if compared to their identity representations. I prefer to spend more time on visiting virtual destinations rather than shopping and this aspect matches my travelling behaviour in actual destinations outside the virtual world. Also, I am not following the virtual gender serotype discussed by Dunn and Guadagno (2012: 106), who claim that 'women were more to invest time [*sic*] in traditional feminine behaviour by focusing on improvements to their appearance'. I am also seeking adventurous activities, such as base jumping and flying, activities that I might never try in my actual life.

Moreover, my religious thoughts and practices, which have been socially constructed during 30 years of my life, influence my behaviour in Second Life. As I mentioned before, a 'proper' Muslim girl should obey her guardians and wear a hijab. Non-mahram people should not see you in improper dress. We were not influenced by Western gender stereotypes but trapped in Islamic gender identities. Unconsciously, I have internalised these practices and I do not 'let my hair down' in public virtual environments. For instance, I am not comfortable wearing bikinis on virtual beaches and I do not do it, despite having this opportunity freely available. It is worth mentioning that I have a chance to fully cover myself with a hijab or to be totally naked but I avoid doing both. As Hans (2007: 4) points out, 'avatars will never be authentic expressions of their creators' true selves'.

Additionally, I am quite a shy person and I carry this personality trait with me during my virtual journeys. My physical features reduce my freedom to act and express myself as a woman in my daily life. However, living in a Muslim patriarchal environment reduced my feminine performances' power in both public and private spheres. Therefore, I accept as 'normal' the fact that I carry my shyness with me in Second Life. I rarely take an initiative to start a conversation but I am open to people if they want to chat with me.

Conclusion

The growing number of netnographic tourism studies in the last decade reveals the importance of the internet as a field of study for many researchers. Netnography is a qualitative methodology that explores culture within an online community. Mkono et al. (2015: 167) claim that netnographic researchers have neglected 'self-refection', 'reflexivity' and 'interrogation of self'. In this respect, autonetnography is an approach that could fill this gap by giving more space for the researchers to tell their own online stories and experiences. Yet, autonetnography has not received attention from tourism scholars.

The present chapter, however, makes a few noteworthy contributions to this methodological approach, virtual tourist experiences and virtual gender identity. Methodologically, it provides an overview of autonetnographic studies in virtual tourism. Furthermore, this chapter contributes to knowledge as it casts light on a researcher's experiences and Iranian Muslim women's virtual tourist journeys in 3D virtual environments. Also, the researcher tried to present a meaningful analysis of her virtual gender identity by providing her lifetime autoethnography.

Netnography and virtual tourism are not new concepts; yet, more research is needed in these areas and on researchers' reflexive approaches. Indeed, more research employing autonetnographic approaches would provide a better understanding of virtual tourist experiences and virtual gender identities, topics that have not been explored by tourism scholars.

References

Arens, W. (1979) *The Man-Eating Myth: Anthropology and Anthropophagy*. New York: Oxford University Press.
Ben-Ze'ev, A. (2004) *Love Online: Emotions on the Internet*. Cambridge: Cambridge University Press.
Bochner, A.P. (2000) Criteria against ourselves. *Qualitative Inquiry* 6 (2), 266–272.
Dunn, R.A. and Guadagno, R.E. (2012) My avatar and me – Gender and personality predictors of avatar–self discrepancy. *Computers in Human Behavior* 28 (1), 97–106. doi:10.1016/j.chb. 2011.08.015.
Eisenchlas, S.A. (2012) Gendered discursive practices on-line. *Journal of Pragmatics* 44 (4), 335–345. doi:10.1016/j.pragma.2012.02.001.
Ellingson, L. and Ellis, C. (2008) Autoethnography as constructionist project. In J.A. Holstein and J.F. Gubrium (eds) *Handbook of Constructionist Research* (pp. 445–466). New York: Guilford Press.
Ellis, C. (2004) *The Ethnographic I: A Methodological Novel About Autoethnography*. Walnut Creek: AltaMira Press.
Fetterman, D.M. (ed.) (2010) *Ethnography: Step-By-Step* (Vol. 17). Thousand Oaks, CA: Sage.
Foucault, M. (1972) *The Archaeology of Knowledge* (translated from the French by A.M. Sheridan Smith). London: Tavistock.
Gilgun, J. (2010) Reflexivity and qualitative research. *Current Issues in Qualitative Research* 1 (2), 1–8.
Hans, G. (2007) Me, myself and my avatar. Some microsociological reflections on 'Second Life'. In *Sociology in Switzerland: Towards Cybersociety and 'Vireal' Social Relations*. Online publication, at http://socio.ch/intcom (accessed May 2016).
Hayano, D. (1979) Auto-ethnography: Paradigms, problems, and prospects. *Human Organization* 38 (1), 99–104. doi: 10.17730/humo.38.1.u761n5601t4g318v.
Herring, S.C. (2000) Gender differences in CMC: Findings and implications. *Computer Professionals for Social Responsibility Journal* 18 (1). doi: 10.1177/107769900608300202.
Herring, S.C. (2004) Computer-mediated discourse analysis: An approach to researching online behavior. In S.A. Barab, R. Kling and J.H. Gray (eds) *Designing for Virtual Communities in the Service of Learning* (pp. 338–376). New York: Cambridge University Press.
Huffaker, D.A. and Calvert, S.L. (2005) Gender, identity, and language use in teenage blogs. *Journal of Computer-Mediated Communication* 10 (2). doi: 10.1111/j.1083-6101.2005.tb00 238.x.
Kottak, C. (1996) *Mirror for Humanity*. New York: McGraw-Hill.
Kozinets, R.V. (2002) The field behind the screen: Using netnography for marketing research in online communities. *Journal of Marketing Research* 39 (1), 61–72.
Kozinets, R.V. (2006) Netnography 2.0. In R.W. Belk (ed.) *Handbook of Qualitative Research Methods in Marketing* (pp. 129–142). Northampton, MA: Edward Elgar.
Kozinets, R.V. (2010) *Netnography*. London: Sage.
Kozinets, R.V. and Kedzior, R. (2009) I, Avatar: Auto-netnographic research in virtual worlds. *Virtual Social Identity and Consumer Behavior* 2, 3–19.
Kuper, A. (1996) *Anthropology and Anthropologists: The Modern British School*. New York: Routledge.
Lévi-Strauss, C. (1968) *Structural Anthropology*. New York: Basic Books.

Lyotard, J.F. (1984) *The Postmodern Condition: A Report on Knowledge* (Vol. 10). Minneapolis, MN: University of Minnesota Press.

Malinowski, B. (1922) *Argonauts of the Western Pacific: An Account of Native Enterprise and Adventure in the Archipelagoes of Melanesian New Guinea*. London: Routledge and Kegan Paul.

Maréchal, G. (2010) Autoethnography. In A.J. Mills, G. Durepos and E. Wiebe (eds) *Encyclopedia of Case Study Research* (Vol. 2, pp. 43–45). Thousand Oaks, CA: Sage.

Mkono, M. (2013) African and Western tourists: Object authenticity quest? *Annals of Tourism Research* 41, 195–214. doi:10.1016/j.annals.2013.01.002.

Mkono, M. and Markwell, K. (2014) The application of netnography in tourism studies. *Annals of Tourism Research* 48, 289–291. doi: 10.1016/j.annals.2014.07.003.

Mkono, M., Ruhanen, L. and Markwell, K. (2015) From netnography to autonetnography in tourism studies. *Annals of Tourism Research* 52, 167–169. doi:10.1016/j.annals.2015.03.002.

Munar, A., Gyimóthy, S. and Cai, L. (2013) *Tourism Social Media: A New Research Agenda* (Tourism Social Science Series, Vol. 18). Bingley: Emerald Group Publishing.

Palomares, N.A. and Lee, E.J. (2010) Virtual gender identity: The linguistic assimilation to gendered avatars in computer-mediated communication. *Journal of Language and Social Psychology* 29 (1) 5–23. doi: 10.1177/ 0261927X09351675.

Richardson, L. (2000) Evaluating ethnography. *Qualitative Inquiry* 6 (2), 253–255.

Schroeder, R. (2002) Social interaction in virtual environments: Key issues, common themes, and a framework for research. In R. Schroeder (ed.) *The Social Life of Avatars: Presence and Interaction in Shared Virtual Environments* (pp. 1–18). New York: Springer-Verlag.

Scott-Jones, J. and Watt, S. (eds) (2010) *Ethnography in Social Science Practice*. New York: Routledge.

Spears, R. and Lea, M. (1994) Panacea or panopticon? The hidden power in computer-mediated communication. *Communication Research* 21 (4), 427–459. doi: 10.1177/00936509402100 4001.

Tavakoli, R. and Mura, P. (2015) 'Journeys in Second Life' – Iranian Muslim women's behaviour in virtual tourist destinations. *Tourism Management* 46, 398–407. doi:10.1016/j.tourman. 2014.07.015.

Tavakoli, R. and Mura, P. (2016) Iranian women traveling: Exploring an unknown universe. In E. Wilson and C. Khoo-Lattimore (eds) *Women and Travel*. Oakville: Apple Academic Press.

9 Conclusion

Paolo Mura and Catheryn Khoo-Lattimore

Writing the concluding remarks for an edited book is far from an easy task. As with many other edited books that consist of chapters written by different authors, this book could be conceived as a fragmented piece of work, in Denzin and Lincoln's (2005) terms a 'quilt' made of different, non-homogeneous patches. We would like to contend, however, that metaphorically this book should be regarded as a mosaic, namely an assemblage of many different types of pieces or *tesserae* that in its entirety provides a cohesive picture of the current scenario of Asian genders in tourism. The fact that the diversity of these tesserae may threaten the cohesiveness of this work has at times been a source of concern for us as editors and contributors. However, as social scientists driven by non-positivist ontologies and epistemologies, we are well aware of the difficulty of (re)producing and (re)presenting the complexity of social 'realities'. Furthermore, as editors, we both believe that there are common threads that weave the various narratives contained in the chapters together, a sort of invisible glue that makes this book an integrated piece of work.

Undoubtedly, this book provides important information about the state of tourism gender research in Asia. We have encountered major obstacles in finding published research and scholars focusing on gender and tourism in Asia, due to the existence of multiple knowledge gaps. First, we need to acknowledge that gender has not received the same attention that other topics have in tourism studies. Without focusing on Asia specifically, Figueroa-Domecq *et al.* (2015: 87) point out that 'despite three decades of study and a recent increase in papers, tourism gender research remains marginal to tourism inquiry'. The marginality of research on gender within tourism studies is particularly pronounced within the context of Asia. In this respect, we hope that this book becomes a vehicle that will drive the tourism academic community to reflect upon the global and local forces that shape the epistemology of tourism knowledge and critically scrutinise why certain tourism topics are privileged over others.

Second, while gender and tourism have been a subject of interest within Western academic circles, less has been written by Asian scholars about Asia. In this regard, we have experienced the struggle of relating the Asian local scenarios to gender theories developed by Western scholars, due to the specificity of Asian socio-cultural contexts. While Figueroa-Domecq et al. (2015) rightly reiterate the existence of 'a male-dominated academic elite' leading tourism academic circles, we would also like to emphasise that a *Western* male-dominated elite plays a hegemonic role in the production of tourism gender research in Asia. In other words, not only have colonial and postcolonial structures of power contributed to reproduce gendered structures of power (as discussed in Yang and Mura's contribution in Chapter 2), they have also played a pivotal role in influencing tourism knowledge creation and legitimation about Asian genders.

It is not surprising, thus, as Yang and Tavakoli discuss in Chapter 3, that the construction of knowledge of Asian and non-Asian genders is mostly the product of female researchers. However, we believe that gender-related inequalities should be a matter of concern for both men and women, as equal societies cannot be constructed without everybody's participation and contribution. In this respect, during the conceptualisation and preparation of this book, we were deliberate in giving voice to both female and male researchers conducting research on gender, despite the paucity of the latter.

Third, we would like to emphasise a point raised by many of our Asian colleagues, which may help us to understand the nature and meanings of the existing knowledge gaps about Asian genders (both in tourism-related disciplines and in other disciplines). Research on gender in Asia does exist but it has not been published in English. As Hall *et al.* point out,

> No matter how important local and national knowledge is, unless it is conveyed in English it has little chance of entering the global marketplace of ideas and be reproduced and recirculated. This does not mean that tourism research in other languages does not have significance; rather, it just means that its international reach is not as great. (Hall *et al.*, 2014: 10)

While the reasons behind the lack of research published in English are multiple, we believe that they cannot transcend the structures of power in which Asian scholars and students are often entangled. Many of our Asian colleagues come from relatively poor economic and social backgrounds, in which the socio-economic gaps between the wealthy and the poor are still pronounced and highly visible. Although the rise of an Asian middle class has been documented in the literature (Kharas, 2010), obtaining an international education in English is still a mirage in many Asian countries. This is especially so in the rural areas of the less developed countries. While globalising forces propel the idea that 'the world is flat' (Friedman, 2005), our daily routines and experiences in Asian countries make us aware that global and local structures of power do not allow many Asian scholars to emerge in the international academic arena.

Another emergent theme highlighted by many of our contributors in their chapters is the difficulty of representing the multiple realities constituting 'Asia'. As ethnicity, religion, history (e.g. colonialism) and globalising forces play a major role in the production of 'maleness' and 'femaleness', we are more comfortable in using the word 'genders' to represent the intricacies of the Asian gendered universe. But in the various chapters, our contributors (Yang & Mura, Chapter 2; Lim & Mura, Chapter 4; Tan & Abu Bakar, Chapter 6) asked themselves some very pertinent questions: Are our own specific experiences representative of all the Asian genders? If so, how? In this regard, we ourselves would readily acknowledge that our tourism journeys and reflections are far from representing all the existing realities of 'Asia' and 'Asianness'. Indeed, we are well aware that our mosaic is only a partial representation or 'preferred view' of the multiple realities of gender and tourism in Asia. Yet, we would like to contend that our experiences and writings, despite being an incomplete representation of gendered tourism experiences in Asia, provide important insights into this unexplored universe, which could pave the way for important reflections about the ontological and epistemological meanings of 'Asia', 'gender' and 'tourism'.

The knowledge gaps discussed above proved to be a source of frustration and stress for all the contributors. How did we overcome all these obstacles? Undoubtedly, embracing reflexivity has played a pivotal role in overcoming the existing gaps in knowledge on gender and tourism in Asia. By reflecting upon our fieldwork and daily routines in Asia, we have attempted to critically examine the meanings of gender in our travelling experiences. As researchers, we have become more aware of the dynamics through which our gendered identities and practices can contribute not only to reiterating but also to challenging the gendered structures of power in Asia. Within the context of this book, contributors have reflected upon their identities and how 'doing fieldwork' with our own gendered bodies constructs gender. For example, the work presented by Lim and Mura (Chapter 4), Rawat and Khoo-Lattimore (Chapter 5) and Tavakoli (Chapter 8) reminds us that discourses concerning women's oppression and men's hegemony do not transcend researchers' experiences and gendered bodies. Tavakoli's work (Chapter 8) shows how reflexivity can be used as a tool to resist gender-based societal constraints. Yang and Mura (Chapter 2) unveil the differences within the various masculinities and femininities. Likewise, Rawat and Khoo-Lattimore (Chapter 5) contend that researchers can be 'privileged' in the field due to their gender.

Overall, all the narratives presented in the chapters allow us to reflect upon the role of tourism in producing, reiterating and resisting existing gendered structures of power in Asia. By encouraging encounters between tourists and locals, tourism spaces are zones of both cohesion and conflict in which gendered structures of power are fluid, (re)invented or simply accepted through performative acts. Within tourism contexts, Asian female hosts and guests are allowed to leave the domestic realm of 'home' and have access to traditionally masculine public spheres (Chapters 2 and 7). However, they cannot totally escape from the gendered stereotypical images of femininity, which often tend to 'construct women' as men's objects of desire. Likewise, hegemonic male identities are questioned in tourism settings (see Chapter 4); yet, they are also reiterated in host–guest interactions (see Chapter 5). This reminds us that gendered structures of power are not fixed but change according to macro-forces (e.g. historical, socio-cultural and political) and micro-forces (the specific socio-cultural tourism setting, the individuality of the particular gendered performance that an individual decides to enact in that specific context) that shape them. Also, whether gendered roles are challenged or reiterated in tourism settings is a matter of researchers' positionality as well as how scholarly production decides to portray gendered relations. As we mentioned earlier, as tourism scholars we play a role in constructing 'genders'.

Avenues for Future Research

This book casts light on Asian genders in tourism. As editors, we believe that we have unveiled some of the intricacies of Asian gendered identities on holiday. Yet, we cannot deny that more research is needed for a better understanding of this unknown universe. More specifically, we would like to encourage more Asian tourism scholars to focus on gender and tourism. While we believe that non-Asian perspectives are important in the understanding of Asian genders, we also contend that Asian scholars' voices need to be heard more loudly in an academic scenario dominated by Western assumptions and paradigms. We would also like to urge our Asian colleagues to publish their work in English. As non-native English speakers ourselves, we acknowledge that this is often easier said than done. However, the wider audience that scholarly production in English can command is important in disseminating and advancing knowledge in this area. At the same time, we would also encourage the Anglo-Saxon world to be more proactive in establishing a dialogue with non-English-speaking academicians, as that would minimise academic structures of power and help to overcome existing knowledge gaps.

References

Denzin, N.K. and Lincoln, Y.S. (2005) Introduction: The discipline and practice of qualitative research. In N.K. Denzin and Y.S. Lincoln (eds) *The Sage Handbook of Qualitative Research* (3rd edn) (pp. 1–43). Thousand Oaks, CA: Sage.

Figueroa-Domecq, C., Pritchard, A., Segovia-Pérez, M., Morgan, N. and Villacé-Molinero, T. (2015) Tourism gender research: A critical accounting. *Annals of Tourism Research* 52, 87–103.

Friedman, T. (2005) *The World Is Flat: A Brief History of the Twenty-First Century*. New York: Farrar, Straus and Giroux.

Hall, C.M., Williams, A.M. and Lew, A.A. (2014) Tourism: Conceptualizations, disciplinarity, institutions, and issues. In A.A. Lew, C.M. Hall and A.M. Williams (eds) *The Wiley Blackwell Companion to Tourism* (pp. 3–24). Chichester: Wiley.

Kharas, H. (2010) *The Emerging Middle Class in Developing Countries* (Working Paper No. 285). Paris: OECD Development Centre.

Index

ABDC List 27, 36
America/American 4, 84, 88, 89, 90, 91, 92, 93, 94, 95, 96, 97, 98, 99, 100, 101, 108
  South Asian American 4, 88, 89, 91, 92, 93, 94, 100
Anglo-America/American 70
  Bangladeshi American 89
  Bengali-American/American 99
  Indian-America/American 92
  North America/American 92, 100,
Asian female tourist gaze 4, 65, 72, 74, 75, 82, 83, 84
Asian female travellers 15, 35, 65, 67, 73
Asian holidays 14
  South Asian holidays 95
Asian masculine identity/identities 13
Asian masculinities 8, 9, 13, 18, 54, 60
Asian scholars 3, 16, 23,25, 29, 30, 32, 35, 36, 41, 42, 53, 122, 123, 124
Asian tourism gender scholars 35
Asian values 9, 76, 83
Asianness 1, 3, 9, 17, 41, 123
Authorship 23, 24, 25, 26, 29, 30
Autoethnography 25, 66, 73, 105, 107, 109, 111, 118
Autonetnography 104, 105, 106, 107, 110, 111, 115, 118
Avatar 116

Body/bodies 2, 11, 12, 40, 41, 42, 43, 44, 45, 47, 48, 49, 51, 74, 93, 98, 116, 117, 123
Buddhism 9, 11, 55, 69, 83

Chinese women 12, 14, 17, 33, 77
Confucianism 2, 8, 9, 69, 80, 83
Corporeality 40, 49, 51
Critical turn in tourism studies 42

Embodiment/embody/embodies 1, 3, 40, 41, 42, 43, 44, 45, 49, 50, 51, 68, 70, 71, 98,116, 117
Ethnic and class inequalities 13
Ethnography 25, 66, 73, 91, 105, 106, 107, 108, 109, 111, 118

Freedom in research 34

Gay Indonesian men 16
Gender oppression 15
Gender research in tourism 6, 24, 25, 32, 53
Gendered division of labour 16
Gendered performances 41, 42, 44, 45, 46, 50
Genders 2, 3, 4, 5, 7, 17, 18, 34, 42, 43, 70, 71, 105, 121, 122, 123, 124

Hegemonic and subordinated 12, 13
Hinduism 2, 9
Home 14, 35, 55, 77, 81, 88, 89, 91, 95, 97, 98, 99, 100, 101, 124

Identities 1, 2, 3, 4, 5, 6, 7, 8, 9, 11, 12, 13, 14, 17, 18, 41, 44, 45, 51, 54, 72, 82, 88, 90,91, 92, 93, 94, 100, 101, 111,112,115, 117, 118, 119, 123,124

Indonesia 8, 11, 16, 26, 44, 56
Interpretive 25, 33, 35, 66, 72, 74
Iran 5, 29, 31, 35, 104, 105, 107, 111, 112, 114, 115, 117, 118
Iranian female travellers 35
Islam 2, 8, 9, 10, 11, 16, 17, 55, 104, 111, 112, 113, 114, 118
Islamic societies 9, 16, 17

Japan 13, 15, 17, 28, 31, 33, 70, 75, 77
Japanese female tourists 15, 33

Malay Muslim women 16
Malaysia 2, 11, 26, 31, 34, 35, 41, 44, 54, 55, 56, 59, 82, 105, 115
Masculinities 3, 4, 8, 9, 13, 14, 15, 16, 17, 18, 31, 34, 53, 54, 57, 60, 123
Methodology 23, 24, 25, 26, 28, 32, 33, 43, 61, 108, 118
Mobile cultural diaspora 88, 97
Muslim women 10, 11, 16, 17, 33, 82, 105, 107, 112, 118
Myanmar 12

Netnography 29, 32, 33, 39, 104, 105, 106, 107, 110, 111, 115, 118

Performance 3, 4, 25, 28, 31, 36, 40, 41, 42, 43, 44, 45, 46, 47, 48, 49, 50, 51, 58, 59, 68, 99, 105, 118, 124
Performativity 3, 41, 42, 43
Physicality 40
Positionality 43, 54, 59, 61, 66, 124
Positivistic quantitative research 35
Postmodern 7, 24, 57, 60, 68, 93
Publications 4, 8, 23, 27, 30

Reflexivity 2, 3, 26, 34, 42, 50, 51, 53, 54, 72, 73, 74, 75, 76, 78, 83, 109, 110, 118, 123
Religion 2, 9, 11, 16, 17, 55, 56, 74, 82, 101, 106, 115, 123

Research topic 23, 24, 25, 26, 27, 28, 30, 31, 32, 34, 35, 42
Researcher–respondent relationship 53, 54, 60, 61

Second Life 104, 105, 111, 115, 116, 117, 118
Singapore 4, 12, 26, 66, 75, 76, 77, 78, 79, 80, 81, 82
Social and cultural construction 11, 70, 75
South Asian American Women 4, 88, 89, 91, 94
South Korea 12, 15
Southeast Asia 1, 8, 9, 10, 11, 13, 15, 16, 23, 26, 32, 41
Southeast Asian women 16
Stage 4, 27, 42, 43, 45, 46, 47, 48, 49, 72, 97

Tanning 42, 43, 45, 46, 47, 48, 49, 50, 51
Thailand 11, 26
Tourism and hospitality education 23
Tourism gender research 23, 25, 26, 30, 37, 121, 122
Tourism research in Asia 1, 3, 26
Tourist gaze 4, 28, 29, 31, 65, 66, 67, 68, 70, 72, 73, 74, 75, 82, 83, 84

Virtual (reality, tourism, travel, behaviour, bodies, tourists) 5, 29, 33, 105, 106, 107, 111, 112, 113, 114, 115, 116, 117, 118

Women 3, 4, 5, 6, 7, 8, 9, 10, 11, 12, 13, 14, 15, 16, 17, 23, 24, 25, 27, 28, 29, 31, 32, 33, 36, 47, 48, 49, 50, 51, 53, 54, 57, 58, 59, 60, 65, 66, 70, 71, 72, 77, 82, 88, 89, 91, 94, 95, 96, 99, 100, 101, 104, 105, 106, 107, 112, 113, 114, 117, 118, 122, 123, 124

For Product Safety Concerns and Information please contact our EU Authorised Representative:

Easy Access System Europe

Mustamäe tee 50

10621 Tallinn

Estonia

gpsr.requests@easproject.com